A Computer Dictionary
for Kids and Other Beginners

A Computer Dictionary
for Kids and Other Beginners

by David Fay Smith

with Commentary by A Board of Children

Amanda Wetherbee Smith   Jared Lynch Smith

Ian Lynch Smith   Colin Lynch Smith

Illustrations by Bill Charmatz

BALLANTINE BOOKS · NEW YORK

Library of Congress Catalog Card Number: 84-90825

ISBN: 345-31693-2

Manufactured in the United States of America

First Edition: August 1984

10   9   8   7   6   5   4   3   2   1

Prepared for publication by The QWERTY Group, Inc., New York

Designed by Irwin Glusker with Sara Jane Goodman

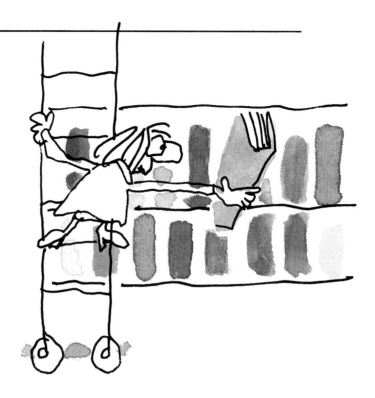

A Note to Parents and Other Beginners

This dictionary was written for children aged eight and up, their parents, and other adults who would like to acquire a working vocabulary of the terms and concepts that surround computers. Margaret Mead wrote that children are the only true citizens of a culture. Whatever technology is current when we are young is "natural" to us. Children are acquiring computer literacy "naturally," the same way we learned automobile, typewriter or vacuum cleaner literacy—by having and using them as a matter of course. But young people need guidebooks to fill in the gaps, and for when no peer is handy. Ian Smith says in his essay on computer camps (page 56), "The best thing about computer camp is always having someone around to answer all the questions you have when you are learning about computers."

Parents who are beginners need guidebooks to help them catch up with the revolution themselves, and to help them translate and amplify for the children. This dictionary is intended to satisfy that need as painlessly as possible by using plain language and common metaphors. You do not have to be a computer expert to be a helpful guide, especially to the young.

Still other beginners are coming to computers on the job. They are finding that even though few applications require advanced computer knowledge, and most demand knowledge only of the task at hand—whether it is writing or financial analysis—the new technology has its own, sometimes obscure vocabulary. This dictionary is for them, too.

In choosing the words to be defined, I selected words and concepts that form a core of understanding, a key vocabulary for beginning a relationship with computers. Generally, I have emphasized personal and home computers, but I have included some words that I wish I had known when I took up with bigger machines, before the small ones were available. I also added some words because they are either interesting in themselves or illustrate a useful point. Jargon is not really a fog developed to confuse outsiders, but a kind of shorthand grabbed from any handy shelf and pressed into service where there is not yet any formal vocabulary to describe a new idea. (Scholars have had a particularly handy shelf for years, called Latin.)

We chose a dictionary format flexible enough to accommodate as much explanation as seemed necessary. Bill Charmatz's illustrations play on the definitions and provide color and energy to encourage browsing—turning the pages just to see what he'll do next.

The Board of Children

I turned to my daughter and three of her lifelong friends for essays to illustrate the different ways in which kids are becoming citizens of a computer culture. When we started this project, Amanda was 13 and in the eighth grade. The other Smith children live two doors down the block. Colin, the oldest, was 17 and a junior in high school. Jared was 14 and Ian was 12. Both families got computers at about the same time in 1980, and there has been a constant flow of programs, hardware and advice between the two households ever since, just as the hand-me-down flotsam and jetsam of their nursery years flowed in years past.

The four kids are strongly individual in their interests and temperaments, and their different experiences and comments reflect a range of reactions to computers. Although not scientifically selected, they do represent a cross section of approaches—from Amanda, who progressed from games to word processing; to Colin, who teaches an afterschool computer course; to Jared, the games master; to Ian, who is already a veteran computer camper and is fast becoming an advanced programmer. For all four, computers are a normal, enjoyable part of ordinary life in a way that their parents' generation, as children, never even dreamed of.

—DFS

Contents

**It's Not Always Your Fault!!!
Or, What You Can Do When
Something Won't Work
by Ian Lynch Smith   page 19**

**The Camp Idlepines Survey:
What Makes Some Girls Like
Computers
by Amanda Wetherbee Smith
page 26**

**Computer Literacy for Pre-
Literates
by Colin Lynch Smith
page 36**

access   Because it means both the ability to approach, or get into, something and the process by which that is done, this word is really what computers are all about. Computers give us access to information. Access is a noun that in computer terminology has been given new meaning as a verb. To access means to enter or gain control of either a particular item of information or a whole system. You access the computer, or access a **file** of information, or access a **disk**.

accumulator   Most computer memory is like a lot of little boxes that can hold only one thing at a time; if you put a new thing in any of the boxes, it replaces or erases what was there before. An accumulator is a special kind of memory that is used for addition and subtraction. Instead of replacing what is in the accumulator, the new number is added to or subtracted from what is already there. (See also **register** and **arithmetic unit**.)

acoustic coupler   Acoustic means having to do with sound. An acoustic coupler is part of a **MODEM**, a device for communicating between computers over phone lines. The coupler uses a pair of rubber cups that fit over the ear and mouthpiece parts of the telephone handset, and it works by transmitting the sounds that are sent back and forth. Other kinds of MODEM can be plugged directly into the phone jack.

Ada   A programming language that was developed by the Department of Defense to give instructions to military computers. It was named after Lady Augusta Ada Lovelace (1815-1852), daughter of Lord Byron, the nineteenth-century English poet. She was a mathematical genius who worked with a man named Charles Babbage on the development of his **Analytical Engine** a little over one hundred years ago. Ada made important contributions to the concepts of programming the Engine and all later computers, including the key idea of using **binary** instead of **decimal** arithmetic. She was the first computer programmer.

address   Computer memories are organized into collections of slots, or pigeonholes, in a very orderly way. Each such memory location can hold one **byte** of information at a time, and each has a number that is its address.

algorithm   Any problem or action can be broken down into a series of small choices that are made in yes-or-no terms, whether it is a method for solving long division or making cookies. (Is the denominator smaller than the first digit of the numerator? If not, is it smaller than the first two digits?, etc. Or, is the measuring cup half full of sugar? If yes, add it to the flour mixture; if not, add more sugar to the measuring cup. Is the oven temperature 325°F? If not, wait one minute. Check the temperature. Is the oven temperature 325°F? If yes, put the cookies in the oven and set the timer, etc.) The set of steps that you go through to solve a particular problem is called an algorithm, and each problem has a different set: the long division algorithm or the cookie algorithm. Problems have to be stated in this boring, step-by-step way for computers because computers work only in **binary**, or yes/no terms. Most problems can have more than one algorithm.

analog   An analog is something that helps us to understand or measure something else. A map is an analog of an area of land. The movement of liquid in a thermometer is an analog of changes in temperature. Computers that measure continuous data—data that may change from minute to minute—are analog computers. The accuracy of their calculations is limited by the precision of the instruments doing the measuring. In contrast, **digital** computers count things and then perform calculations of extreme accuracy and precision. Most computers are digital.

Analytical Engine   A device designed in 1833 by Charles Babbage, in England. It was a steam-driven, mechanical device that was too complicated for the mechanical skills of that time, and so it was never completed. But its design included all of the main parts that any computer must have: **input** device, stored **programs**, a **central processing unit**, and an **output** device. Babbage worked on it for more than 20 years, helped by Lady Augusta **Ada** Lovelace, one of the finest mathematicians of the time.

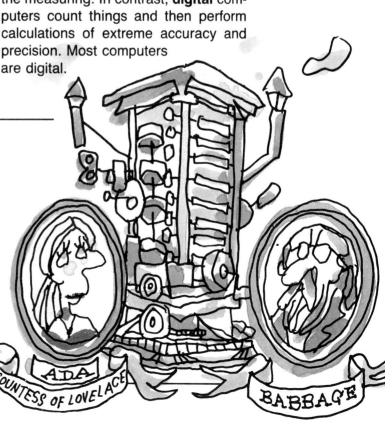

APL   Stands for A Programming Language. APL uses a special set of symbols instead of letters of the alphabet. Because each symbol has a particular meaning that would otherwise have to be spelled out, you can give the computer more instructions in less space than with other languages. Sometimes as many as twenty lines of **BASIC** can be replaced with a single line of APL code.

Apple   The name of one of the most popular personal computers. The best-known models are the Apple II Plus and the newer Apple IIe. They both use the same **microprocessor chip**, and programs that will run on one generally will run on the other. Perhaps Apple's most revolutionary contributions to the microcomputer industry were to design a computer with **expansion slots** so that additional **hardware** could be easily added, and to publish the detailed specifications of the computer so that others could design new hardware and **software** products to go with it. This "open box" approach had a lot to do with the extremely rapid growth of the industry after the first Apples appeared in 1977.

argument   Many commands and instructions in computer programs require some extra information to be supplied. The extra information is called the argument. Word processing programs usually have a way to find any given word or phrase in the text you have entered. The command might be "FIND." The argument would be the word or phrase you want to find.

arithmetic unit   Part of the computer that is used for arithmetic functions, including the **accumulator**. It is usually combined with a section that deals with logic; together they are called the "arithmetic and logic unit," or ALU.

array   A calendar is an array of days. A crossword puzzle is an array of letters and spaces. A chessboard is an array of possible locations for chessmen. An array, then, is an orderly arrangement of data or of spaces for data, usually in rows or in rows and columns. Computers process information one item at a time. Frequently, the results are stored temporarily in arrays that have been defined in the computer's memory, and then printed out only when the processing has been completed. In addition, once an array has been set up, its contents can be referred to or addressed by location. For instance, B(6) could stand for the sixth item in row B. An array is frequently a single string or row of numbers. (See also **matrix**.)

artificial intelligence (AI) The art and science of teaching computers to think or mimic thinking. There is a lot of disagreement about just what intelligence really is, but one direction AI is taking is to mimic special human skills. In terms of general knowledge or common sense, which are incredibly hard to write programs for, there has not been very much progress yet. You can take one look at a toy train and know (or instantly make a good guess at) what the other side of it looks like, what it is made of, whether is is electric, battery-operated, wind-up, remote-controlled, or just pushable, and even whether it is likely to be cheap or expensive. Those guesses are based on a lot of very small bits of knowledge that your brain can quickly organize and use to make fair guesses about many things you have never seen before. Computers are not yet very good at this sort of thing. But in some areas of knowledge that are based on large numbers of facts and rules, such as chess playing and the diagnosis of certain diseases, computers can already outperform most humans.

ASCII Stands for American Standard Code for Information Interchange, pronounced "as-key." It is an agreed-upon code for representing each letter and number in **binary** code. It is one of two generally accepted methods for translating into binary. The other one is called **EBCDIC**, for Extended Binary Coded Decimal Interchange Code, and is used mostly on **IBM** equipment.

---

assembler A program that converts **assembly language** into **machine code** or **object code**. Assembly language is only one small step up from the binary stream of 1's and 0's, but it still has to be interpreted for the computer to be able to use it.

---

assembly language There are many different computer languages, and each one is intended to make using computers more effective in one way or another. Some are close to English in their grammar and syntax, and some are closer to the native language of computers, called **binary code** or **machine code**, which consists of just strings of 1's and 0's. Assembly is one step up from binary. It is complicated to learn, but since it needs very little interpretation for the computer to understand it, it is fast and efficient.

---

asynchronous Describes transmission of data, usually by phone, in which the intervals between groups of data are controlled by the insertion of special **stop bits**. It is used mostly in slow-speed transmissions (up to 1200 **baud**).

background Larger computers are often able to do more than one thing at a time. That capacity is often split between **foreground**, where interaction between the user and the computer is important and the results are needed immediately, and background, where a job can be set up to **run** a little bit at a time, whenever the computer is not busy with foreground work.

backup You should never, never, never permit information or a program that is important to you to exist in only one copy, especially if it is on a **diskette** or other magnetic memory system. Always have a second, backup diskette stored safely away, and a paper printout whenever possible. Computer memories are wonderfully flexible, but they can be destroyed in a trice, through carelessness or just bad luck. Diskettes can last for years, and then suddenly fail, and when they fail it tends to be total rather than gradual. You will experience this problem. Sooner or later every computer user does. But you can limit the damage with backups.

BASIC Stands for Beginners All-purpose Symbolic Instruction Code. It is the most popular of the **high-level languages** for microcomputers because you can easily learn enough of it to gain an understanding of how computers work, and it is powerful enough for you to tackle serious problems with. Developed at Dartmouth College in the early 1960s for people who were not computer specialists, BASIC uses English-like expressions and understandable arithmetic and algebraic notation. It does not look very much like English, but the logic of a BASIC program can be puzzled out with some effort by a relative beginner, which cannot be done with **machine language** or with **assembly language**. Not all BASICs are alike. They vary in their syntax and capabilities according to the machines they are running on, but usually it is possible to convert from one to another by retyping certain kinds of statements in a slightly different form. BASIC is accompanied in the computer by a program called an **interpreter**, which you generally do not even know is there. When you run a BASIC program, the interpreter reads each line of BASIC instruction and converts it into machine language, which the computer can then follow. The program is interpreted each time it is run. (See also **compile**.)

batch processing Setting up computer jobs so that they can be processed without human supervision. Batch processing makes sense when the job requires large amounts of computer power and time, such as processing a payroll for a big manufacturing firm. Batch processing is usually done on large computer **mainframes**. (See also **background**.)

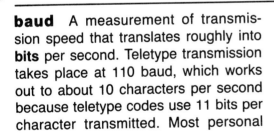

baud A measurement of transmission speed that translates roughly into **bits** per second. Teletype transmission takes place at 110 baud, which works out to about 10 characters per second because teletype codes use 11 bits per character transmitted. Most personal computer telecommunications take place at 300 baud, or about 30 characters per second, and some at 1200 baud. Special equipment and phone lines are needed for rates over 1200 baud.

benchmark A way of comparing the performance of different machines by giving them each the same task to do, and recording their results at various stages. Different computers are good at different tasks. One will be faster going to and from memory, and another will have a faster processor or **arithmetic unit**. To choose a computer for an important application, a **systems analyst** might prepare a program that tests for the features that are particularly important for that application, and then run it on each machine being considered.

binary A bicycle has two wheels. Binoculars have two lenses. Bicentennial means two centuries. Binary means having two parts. All computers use only two simple numbers, 1 and 0, when they are working or talking to each other, but by combining 1's and 0's into groups of eight, any number or letter or arithmetic function can be expressed. Computers use this kind of code because their memories are all based on nothing more than lots of tiny switches that each have only two positions, either on or off. On equals 1; off equals 0. Within a group of eight switches, you can have 2 X 2 X 2 X 2 X 2 X 2 X 2 X 2 = 256 different combinations. That is enough to use one for each letter of the alphabet, including all of the capital letters, the numbers 0 through 9, and all of the symbols like ? ! % & ' ( ) :, plus a lot of extras. One switch is called a **bit** and a set of eight is usually called a **byte**. In fact, in a byte, it is normal for only seven bits (128 combinations) to be used for data and the eighth for padding. (See also **stop bit**.) There are two different systems for representing letters and numbers in binary code, **ASCII** and **EBCDIC**. ASCII is most common on smaller computers, EBCDIC on larger equipment, especially IBMs.

bit Stands for binary digit. It is the smallest unit of information in computers, and it represents one switch that can be either on or off. Bits are usually grouped into packages of eight, called **bytes**.

black box A device that permits one piece of electronic equipment to talk to another, usually by simply plugging cables from both into it. It contains circuits, and perhaps even a **microprocessor** of its own, to translate signals from one into terms that the other can use. It is called a black box because just how it actually works is often a mystery to its user. In some cases, such as military message encoding and decoding ma-chines, the user is not even supposed to know how it works, and that is probably the origin of the term. (See also **interface**.)

Boolean George Boole developed the theoretical link between language and mathematics that finally enabled logicians, and later programmers, to reduce almost any statement or problem to a series of "true" and "not true" statements, which is a kind of **binary** representation that has come to be called Boolean Logic. Boole was British, a self-taught linguist and mathematician. His most important work was published in 1854.

boot Means, "Put the disk (or cartridge or cassette) into the computer and turn it on." It comes from the word bootstrap. Bootstraps are the little tabs inside cowboy boots that are used to pull them on with, and so bootstrapping means to start something without any help, as if you were to reach down and pick yourself right up by pulling hard on those little tabs. It can't be done. But in computers, it means to load a simple program that, in turn, does some more complicated things to get the computer ready to use. Often, the bootstrap program is built right in so that it automatically runs whenever the computer is turned on.

branch Many programs resemble trees when they are diagrammed, with each choice looking like a branch. In a program, any instruction that has the effect of skipping over the next section of code is called a branch.

break A special key on some computer terminals. It has the effect of stopping whatever program is running, and getting the computer ready to do something else or to go back to the beginning of the existing program.

buffer A storage device or space set aside in the main memory of the computer to hold data temporarily, just as a reservoir stores rainwater. If one part of the computer is sending data faster than another part (such as a printer) can receive it, the data can be accumulated in the buffer until the other part can catch up.

bug A bug is an error in a program that makes the computer do something unexpected or not work at all. The term comes from an experience with one of the early computers that used a lot of delicate mechanical parts. A moth got stuck in the works and had to be removed before the computer would work again. **Debugging** is the process of testing programs to find and fix mistakes.

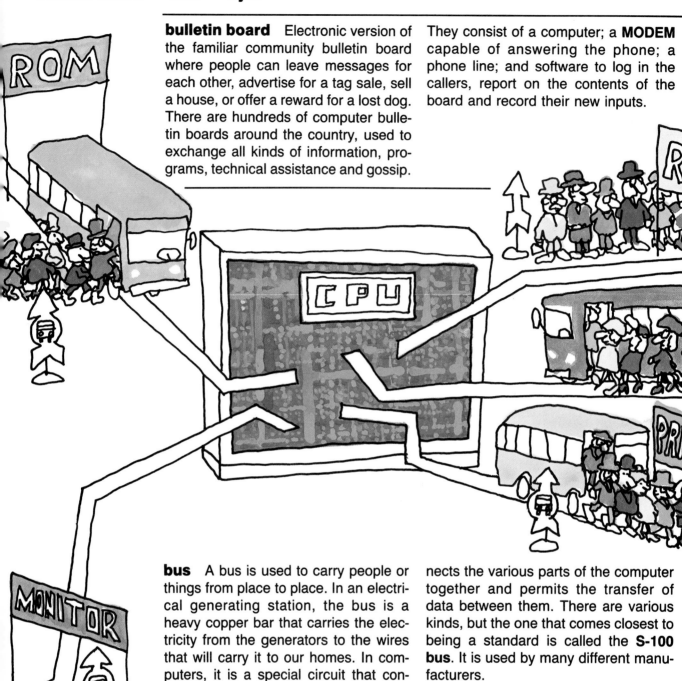

bulletin board Electronic version of the familiar community bulletin board where people can leave messages for each other, advertise for a tag sale, sell a house, or offer a reward for a lost dog. There are hundreds of computer bulletin boards around the country, used to exchange all kinds of information, programs, technical assistance and gossip. They consist of a computer; a **MODEM** capable of answering the phone; a phone line; and software to log in the callers, report on the contents of the board and record their new inputs.

bus A bus is used to carry people or things from place to place. In an electrical generating station, the bus is a heavy copper bar that carries the electricity from the generators to the wires that will carry it to our homes. In computers, it is a special circuit that connects the various parts of the computer together and permits the transfer of data between them. There are various kinds, but the one that comes closest to being a standard is called the **S-100 bus**. It is used by many different manufacturers.

byte A byte is a group of (usually) eight **bits**. Since each bit is a switch that can only be either on or off, each bit can have two states. Eight bits can be arranged in exactly 256 different combinations of on and off, which means that one byte can be set to mean any of 256 different characters, symbols or numbers in **binary** form. Thus, one byte is generally thought of as the equivalent of one character or digit. The word "byte," then, takes four bytes to encode, and a manuscript of 10,000 characters will need 10,000 bytes of memory to hold it. Some larger computers use groups of 16 or 32 bits as their basic units of information, but these larger groups of bits are usually called **words**.

It's Not Always Your Fault!!!
Or, What You Can Try When Something Won't Work

Do you have brothers who constantly blame you for everything? Sometimes it seems that way when you're the youngest. I'll give you an example. Yesterday my brother was at the computer doing a real important paper for school. When he was ready to print, he turned the printer on, but it wouldn't move and it made an awful groaning noise. Naturally, he yelled for me because I was the last one to use it. I came running pretty fast because he can really yell.

Well, I looked at the printer and tried all of the usual things, like turning it off and on, taking it off-line, and checking the way the paper was feeding into the back of the printer through the slot in the table. Everything looked fine but it still didn't work, and I was beginning to think I had really totaled it, when I looked under the desk at the box of printing paper. There was my cat, sound asleep in the box. No wonder the printer was making such a noise. It was trying to print out a 20-pound cat!

I guess the moral of this is, don't panic. Check everything, and don't forget to look for something silly. Here is a list of some silly things to try if your computer doesn't work.

1. If nothing happens when you turn it on, make sure all of the plugs are plugged into the right places, according to the instructions. Be sure that there really is electricity at the wall plug by plugging in a lamp or something.

2. Make sure that your monitor or TV is turned on. Try the brightness and contrast controls. Either one can make the screen look dead.

3. If you have glitches sometimes that make your computer seem to die suddenly in the middle of what you are doing, the reason may be your power supply. The computer may be on a circuit with an air conditioner or washing machine that's causing the power to jiggle. You can get a "surge suppressor" from your dealer that will cure this problem. If the power is OK, you may be getting some static electricity from the rug or the chair you are sitting on. The cheapest way to fix this problem is to use some anti-static spray on the rug, chair, and desk once every few months. Your dealer has it.

4. New floppies have to be formatted or initialized before they can be used. If you can't seem to save something onto a floppy, maybe it hasn't been initialized. Keep a few extra initialized disks on hand.

5. If you accidently erase or delete something you wanted to keep, don't despair. Your dealer probably has a program that will get that file back if you have not written something else over it. He'll sell it to you, or if he is a decent guy, he might occasionally help you out for free. Try to make friends with your dealer. But you are out of luck if you have re-initialized the disk. That erases everything!

6. If your printer is printing double space when you think it should print single, look in its manual for a way to turn off its line feed, or in the program manual for a way to turn off the computer's line feed–but not both.

Read your manuals. They seem pretty boring until you have a problem, and then it helps to know where to look for the answers.

—Ian

CAD/CAM Stands for Computer-Assisted-Design/Computer-Assisted Manufacture. CAD refers to a group of programs that are used by architects and engineers to help draw parts that are to be built. CAM refers to programs that tell machines what to do in the manufacturing process. The two kinds of programs are related: what is designed with the help of a computer is often manufactured with the help of one.

CALL This is a programming statement that sends the program to a separate program or **subroutine** that might be used over and over in different parts of the main program. Using a CALL saves having to write that part of the program each time. In the BASIC language, this function is usually handled by a **GOTO** or **GOSUB** statement. Languages like **FORTRAN** permit CALLs to subroutines that exist as self-contained program segments that can be used by different programs.

---

card Punched cards are an early form of data storage that is still in wide use today. The most common type is 7¾ by 3⅛ inches, with 80 columns of 12 rows each. One hole is punched in each column to represent one digit (0 - 9), while letters take two or more positions in a column. Herman Hollerith developed the idea to help tabulate the results of the 1890 U.S. Census. The 1880 census had taken eight years to tabulate by hand. With Hollerith's invention, the 1890 census count took one month, and the whole process was completed in three years. Hollerith later set up a tabulating machine company that in 1924 became International Business Machine Corporation, and later, IBM. Many conventions of computer design, such as 80- and 40-column **monitor**screens can be traced to the design of punched cards.

catalog A list of contents, particularly of a disk or some other storage medium. To catalog a disk is to instruct the computer to print out a list of all of the files on the disk. The command is usually "CAT" or "CATALOG," followed by the name or number of the disk if there is more than one.

Cathode Ray Tube (CRT) The kind of tube that forms the viewing screen used in TVs and **monitors**. Often, the term CRT is used to mean any and all kinds of video display, including the keyboard that goes with it, making the term almost interchangeable with **terminal**. Another term is VDU, for Video Display Unit.

Central Processing Unit (CPU) This is the heart of the computer, where all of the calculations take place. In a microcimputer, it is the microprocessor chip, a 6502 in an Apple or a Pet, a Z-80 in a TRS-80, and Intel 8088 in the IBM Personal Computer.

character set Means the set of characters—letters and symbols—that are available for display or printing. One printer's character set, for example, might include special scientific symbols, or accent marks for French, or the upside-down question mark used in Spanish.

chip The chip is a tiny sliver of pure silicon that is used to hold the many circuits and transistors that make up a microprocessor or memory device. The tiny components are etched on the silicon using photographic processes, and the result is called an integrated circuit. The first of these included some dozens of transistors on one chip. When the number of transistors on a chip got into the hundreds, the process was called large-scale integration (LSI). Now there can be thousands of transistors and circuits on a single chip, and that process is called very large scale integration (**VLSI**).

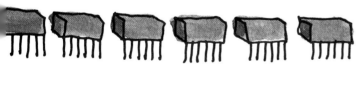

clock There are two kinds of clocks to consider. The first kind is an electronic device that generates pulses at a rate of (usually) between 1 and 8 million per second (megahertz). The computer uses the timing of these pulses to synchronize all of its internal workings. Every computer must have this kind of clock. The second kind of clock does something more familiar: it tells time, and it is optional. If your computer has a timekeeping clock, it can be used to turn appliances on and off (including the computer itself), to make calls at special times for transferring data by phone, and to keep track of all of your files and programs according to the date and time of day they were last changed.

CLOSE A programming command to close a file or files that had been previously **OPEN**ed. Programs must frequently get information from **files** and put corrected or additional information in them. Just as you do with a traditional file folder, the program must open a file before it can read or write in it, and it must close that file before going on to the next part of the job, or risk losing the contents of the file.

C-MOS Stands for Complementary Metal Oxide **Semiconductor**, a kind of semiconductor that needs very little power and is stable over a wide range of temperatures. It is often used in electronic watches, among other things. (See also **MOS.**)

coaxial cable Two electrical conductors sharing the same axis, or core, one wire arranged to shield or surround the other. Usually, "coax" has copper conductor at its core, surrounded by insulation. The ground wire, or shield, is woven around the insulated core, and another layer of insulation completes the cable. Coax is used for communications connections between different pieces of equipment, rather than for electrical power connections. The connection between your computer and TV or monitor is coax. So are the lines that connect your tape deck, phonograph and amplifier together. Other types of connections are called **ribbons** and **twisted pairs**.

COBOL Stands for COmmon Business Oriented Language. COBOL is a **high-level language** like BASIC, except that it is especially useful for business applications like accounting. It uses a lot of English-language statements like "ADD R TO S," where another language might say the same thing with "S = S + R." It takes longer to write a program in COBOL than in some other languages, but it is actually very efficient, once it has been **compiled** into **machine code**.

collate To put things in a certain order. Alphabetical and numerical order are the most common. Collation is one of the most boring activities for a human to do, and therefore one of the most useful kinds of things for a computer to do. (See also **sort**.)

compile Computers understand only machine language, which is hard for humans to write and understand. Several high-level languages, such as **APL, BASIC, COBOL,** and **FORTRAN**, have been developed to make programming easier. Each of these languages uses a special program that translates our program statements from the high-level language that we can understand into the machine language that the computer can understand. There are two kinds of translating programs—compilers and **interpreters**. To compile is to run the compiler program, which reads our program (called **source code**) and translates the whole thing into machine language (called **object code**). Then you can save the compiled version of the program under a new name, and run it instead of the source code. If you have to make a change in the program, you modify the source code and recompile. Most languages use compilers. BASIC, however, usually uses an **interpreter**, which translates the program line by line, executing each line of instructions as it goes. Compiled programs usually run much faster than interpreted programs, but the compiler takes up a lot of memory. That's one of the reasons BASIC is so common on small computers with limited memories.

CompuServe The name of one of the major **timesharing networks** used by individuals as well as businesses. Using a **MODEM**, you can hook up your computer to the big ones that CompuServe has, and exchange information and programs, leave messages, or just chat with other users all over the country. You can also write programs, do word processing, search an encyclopedia, buy a TV, or just play games. The other major service used by individuals is called **The Source**.

concatenate To connect two strings of characters or numbers together and treat them as one.

conditional The command "**IF**" is a conditional. One of the most important parts of programming is the process of checking to see whether a certain condition is present and then taking some action depending on the answer. If I have $100 in my checking account and I want to write a check for a certain amount, my checkbook program should first ask me how big a check I want to write and and then compare that amount to the balance. IF the amount of the check is greater than the balance, the program could print something clever, like "BOUNCE, BOUNCE, BOUNCE," or something more useful like "YOU ARE SHORT BY $X," and then put the difference between my balance and my check in place of X. If the amount of the check is less than or equal to the balance, it might say, "YOUR REMAINING BALANCE WILL BE $X," and then print the new balance in place of X. IF statements are the bread and butter of programming because they make it possible for us and the computer to express problems in true or false, yes or no, **binary** terms.

configure Sometimes an appliance such as an air conditioner or a clothes dryer will work on either ordinary house current (115 volts), or on a special circuit at 220 volts, if you have it available. When the appliance is installed, you configure it for your type of electricity by setting a switch that is usually inside the appliance, since you have to set it only one time. Similarly, with computers, configure means to assemble a selection of **hardware** and **software** into a system and to adjust each of the parts so that they all work together. It can also mean to adjust a piece of software so that it will work with a particular computer configuration.

connect time The time you spend using a **timesharing computer**. It matters in commercial timesharing because it is one of the ways in which you are charged for the use of the computer. Personal computers are splendidly uncaring about connect time; you can use them all day long without having to worry about the meter running. Connect time also refers to the amount of time any two computers are connected together, usually by means of **MODEMs**.

control characters Control characters are special codes that can be typed on the keyboard but that do not result in anything's being printed. Instead, they tell the computer to do special things like ringing bells or moving the cursor around on the screen. The control key on the keyboard is like the shift key on a typewriter. It determines whether other keys will print lower case or capital letters, but it does not print anything itself. Instead of sending the computer the ASCII code for a capital A, for example, the control key and the 'A' send a nonprinting code when pressed together. Control characters can be used in many different ways, depending on how the programmer wants the program to work: they can make the printer skip a page, make the cursor skip a line or delete a whole paragraph. CONTROL is usually abbreviated "CTRL."

core Core is an old-fashioned (before about 1975) term for a computer's internal memory, what we now call **RAM**. It consists of rows and rows of tiny ferrite (iron) doughnuts strung on fine wire in flat racks, several thousand of them in a few square inches. The wires are strung from side to side on the racks, and from top to bottom, forming a grid, with a doughnut at each place where the wires cross. Each intersection can be addressed individually by applying a small current to one side-to-side wire and one top-to-bottom wire, thus changing the magnetic field of the bit of iron at that one intersection. Since it leaves all of the other intersections alone, it is true random access memory—meaning you can enter data at any point. Core memories are still in use in some older computers, and some programmers use the term "core" interchangeably with the word "RAM," although RAM usually implies a chip.

CP/M Stands for Control Program/Microcomputers. Every computer must have an **operating system**. The operating system is a program that keeps track of the transfer of data between the computer's main memory and its disk drives and other attachments. It also determines how information is stored on the disks. Unfortunately, information stored under one operating system usually cannot be used with another. CP/M is one of the most popular operating systems, and many computer manufacturers have designed their machines to use it in order to take advantage of the large number of programs that have been written for it. Apples, TRS-80s and IBM PCs all have their own operating systems, but each of them can be modified to use CP/M as well. It was designed by a company called Digital Research Corporation.

cps Stands for characters per second, usually used in discussions about printing speed. **Dot matrix** printers whizz along at from 80 to 160 cps, while **daisy wheel** printers usually make between 14 and 30 cps. (See also **baud**.)

crash A term used to describe the failure of a computer system or sometimes a program. A head crash is one kind of **hard disk** failure, usually caused by the **head** running into some insurmountably large obstruction, like a mote of dust or a fingerprint.

crosstalk You have probably had the experience of calling someone on the telephone and hearing one or both sides of someone else's separate conversation going on while you were talking. That is crosstalk. It is not supposed to happen, but it sometimes does when wires are bundled too closely together. In computers, crosstalk shows up as interference or electronic noise when one circuit interferes with another. Some kinds of communications wire are man-

ufactured so that pairs twist around each other, called **twisted pairs**, just to minimize the chances of having the wires of different circuits close enough together over a long enough stretch to permit crosstalk.

---

cursor   The cursor is the little blinking light that tells you where the action is taking place on the computer's **monitor** or TV screen. The cursor is the computer's way of showing you where to begin to **input** data or responses for all kinds of programs—word processing, database management, games, etc.

The Camp Idlepines Survey:
What makes some girls like computers?

I have been going to Camp Idlepines for four years now. The camp is located on the outskirts of an out-of-the-way little town called Strafford-Bow Lake, which is somewhere near Concord, NH. Don't be surprised if you've never heard of it, because even someone who got straight A's in geography probably wouldn't know about it. It's a regular summer camp, with swimming, horseback riding, crafts, and campfire singing, but no computers. This year, since my father was in the middle of a computer dictionary, he asked me to do a survey of how Camp Idlepines girls and counselors feel about computers. I said sure, so the day I received the surveys in the mail, I went to the camp director and told her about it. She said I could do the survey at rest hour, when all the campers were in their cabins, and I could talk to them in small groups.

I handed the survey out to all of my cabin first, since they were the oldest (13-14) and the most conveniently located, and told them to fill out the questionnaires and give them to me after rest hour. Then I went to the next cabin, who were the eleven- and twelve-year-olds. I explained to them what I wanted, and then passed out the questionnaires. Most of them took it to their beds, sat down and did it without a problem, but a couple of them sat right by me and asked things like, "Does an Atari game system count as a computer?" (to which the answer was no) and "How am I supposed to know how many kids there are in my school?" Even going to the younger cabins (7-10), I got it done in one rest hour, and in all, I passed out 38 questionnaires to campers and staff, and I got them all back. That's because they were a captive audience.

Then came the next step, analyzing the data.

Three interesting results attracted us. The first was about mothers and computers. We asked the girls to say how enthusiastic they were about computers on a scale of one to five. Twelve said they liked computers "a lot"—the top of the scale. Out of these, nine had computers at home. Eight of these nine said that their mother was a main user of the computer. In the ninth case, the exception, the Idlepiner herself and her father were the main users. In the four families where only the fathers or brothers were main users, the girls were not as enthusiastic. From this we conclude that female role models are important in motivating girls to enjoy using computers.

The next finding is that the age that a person is when her school introduces computers can affect how enthusiastic she becomes. In our survey, the girls who were twelve and under when computers first entered their schools were the most enthusiastic. Of the girls who were over twelve, only one was really enthusiastic. It may mean that girls take to computers very well during the tomboy stage. I know that I did.

The third and most complicated result was about how girls and boys compare in skill at computer strategy games. We asked the Idlepiners whether or not they played strategy games and how well they did, compared to boys. We also asked how well they thought girls in general did, compared to boys. Eight out of the ten girls who said that they play strategy games themselves believe that they are either as good as or better than boys. The girls who had no experience with the computer games were more likely to think that boys would be better at them. We think this is evidence that actual exposure to computer strategy games (not to mention other things such as math and sports) tends to break down the popular stereotypes which say that boys are better than girls—or at least have a natural tendency to be better—at such things. These stereotypes may discourage girls from trying things that they might turn out to be good at if they would give themselves a chance.

—Amanda

daisy wheel A popular kind of **letter-quality** printing technique that uses a disk with flat spokes sticking out around its edge, like the petals on a daisy. A different letter is embossed at the end of each spoke, or petal, and the wheel spins at high speed in front of the paper in the printer. A hammer strikes the letter to be printed as it spins by. The quality of the print can be excellent at printing speeds up to about 30 **cps.**

data Data is the plural form of the Latin word *datum.* Sometimes you will see it used in the plural, as in "These data are dirty," and sometimes you will see it used as a singular noun, as in "This data is very revealing." Both forms are acceptable. Data is/are information. All software is data, but a distinction is usually made between software meaning programs or computer instructions, and software meaning information that the computer needs in order to carry out the instructions it has been given. For example, a program designed to help forecast the weather would need a great deal of data about today's temperature, rainfall, barometric pressure, wind speed and direction, etc., in order to do the calculations that would give a forecast.

database A database is any collection of data. Your address book is a database. So is a list of the clothes you own. So is a collection of stubs from a checkbook or a stack of receipts from the grocery store. It is a collection of bits of information (data) that fit together in some way, or that have something in common. Once these elements are in a computer memory, they can be arranged in many different ways. For instance, your address book would usually be arranged alphabetically by last name, but you might also want to **sort** it by zip code or first name or by the date you last spoke to each person.

data entry The process of putting data into the computer, often in the format of a particular **database**. Data entry can also refer to **input** to word processing programs and spreadsheet programs like **VisiCalc**. The data entry can take place at a computer **terminal's** keyboard, or from **cards** or **tape** or other device.

DBMS Stands for DataBase Management Systems, a class of programs used for managing generally large collections of information. An airline reservation system is an example of a really large DBMS, since it must keep track of every seat on every flight from the present moment until several months into the future, in order to be able to tell a travel agent whether you can reserve seats for your trip to Florida in February.

debug **Bugs** are errors in programs. Debugging is the process of finding mistakes and rewriting the program to get rid of them. Debugging complex programs means testing them over and over again so that every possible combination of data that they might be asked to work with will be handled correctly.

decimal Our familiar numbering system, using base ten, i.e., ten digits, 0 - 9. Other common numbering systems used by computers are **binary** (base 2), **octal** (base 8), and **hexadecimal** (base 16).

decrement The amount by which some value is reduced. Used as a verb, it means to reduce a value by a regular amount, often 1, as in counting down before the blast-off of a spaceship. It is the opposite of **increment**.

default Every question gets an answer of some kind. Even if there is no answer given, the lack of an answer is a kind of information. A default is what the computer assumes is the user's choice if the user does not answer in any other way. (See also **parameter**.)

delete To remove or erase data from a file, or whole programs and files from storage. Once deleted, a file is usually gone for good, so be careful! (But see also **restore**.)

delimiter A symbol that separates one item from the next. The most common delimiter is a comma, as in "2,4,6,8." Some others are parentheses, brackets, braces, and angles.

demodulate To process a signal received over a telephone line so that the computer is able to read it. Such signals are **modulated** at their origins and demodulated at their destinations by devices called **MODEMs.**

Dialog The name of a program for **searching** large **databases**, particularly databases of scientific and technical literature. Dialog Information Services, Inc., offers access to more than 170 such collections using the Dialog software.

digital Using numbers to measure and show results. In the case of a clock with hands, which is an **analog** device, the power of a spring or electricity is translated through a series of gears or a special motor so that the hands move around the clock face at a certain speed. The numbers are spaced to represent hours of the day, so that a glance at the clock will tell you the time. Precision depends on how accurately the speed of the hands is controlled and how much detail is printed on the clock face. In a digital clock a battery supplies power to a tiny computer that produces a constant, very rapid signal that it then counts: so many beats to the second, so many to the minute, etc. These measurements are then shown on the clock's display in numbers, and since the computer is counting very small fractions of a second anyway, it is not difficult to show tenths, hundredths or even thousandths of a second. Most computers work with digital data, usually in **binary** form.

DIP switch Stands for Dual Inline Package, a special kind of **chip** that has a row of little switches on its surface. These are used to **configure** a piece of hardware—a printer, MODEM or the computer itself—to behave in a certain way every time it is used. DIP switches are used instead of **software** control to set **defaults** in situations where the conditions of use are not likely to change very often. Some kinds of printers are capable of printing Japanese characters, for example, but setting them up for it requires setting a DIP switch.

disassemble Machine language is the native language of computers and consists of strings of **binary** code—1's and 0's. It is nearly impossible to decipher. To disassemble is to read the machine language with a program and convert it into **assembly language**, which consists of a series of letter and word codes that are at least somewhat easier to understand. It is not for the faint of heart.

disk Disks are the currently the best way of storing the digital information that computers use to record both programs and data. There are two main types—**hard disks** (including **Winchesters**) and **floppy disks** (or **diskettes**). Disks all have some things in common: they look a bit like phonograph records; they spin on something like a turntable; and the data, like music, is read by a device that moves across their surfaces. But although the phonograph record spins at a rate of 33⅓ revolutions per minute (rpm), a computer disk might spin at up to several thousand rpm. On a phonograph record, the music is recorded in a single long spiral groove, but on a disk, the data is recorded in a series of concentric **tracks** or circles like those on a target, but which are very small and very close together. Instead of in a groove, the data is recorded on a flat surface with a magnetic coating on it similar to the tape in a cassette, and instead of a needle, the disk player, or **disk drive**, uses a tiny magnet, much like the play/record heads on a cassette player. The **head** travels rapidly back and forth from the center to the edge of the disk's surface, and since the disk is spinning so rapidly itself, it is easy to see that every part of every track will pass beneath the head quite often. Therefore, the time needed to find any particular piece of information will be quite short. This is the great advantage of disk over tape. The computer can go directly and very quickly to any part of the disk's surface and either read what is there or write something new in that space, according to the computer's instructions. This process is called **random access**.

disk drive The device that stores and retrieves information from **disks** or **diskettes**. A disk drive for a personal computer is about the size of a small shoe box. For a large computer, several disks might be used at the same time in a machine about the size of jukebox.

diskette A thin disk of flexible plastic with a magnetic coating like that on recording tape. Also called **floppy disks** or just "floppies," diskettes are used for recording **programs** and **data** for computers. They are much cheaper than **hard disks**, but they are slower and they can hold much less information. Diskettes come in square, stiff jackets with holes in them for the **disk drive** to work through. The jackets are there to protect the surface of the disks and are never taken off. The most common size for personal computers is 5¼ inches in diameter. Business computers often use an 8-inch size, and there are also some new sizes available that are 3½ inches in diameter or less, housed in a rigid plastic sleeve. These are called microfloppies. There are many different methods for storing data on the disks, so their capacities range from about 100,000 bytes (100 kilobytes) on one side, up to several megabytes (millions of bytes), using both sides.

Distributed Data Processing (DDP) The concept of having the computer processing take place at or near the places where the data for a project is coming from or being used, rather than at a remote site where the operators may know a lot about computers but not much about the project.

document A **file** in computer memory. It comes from the ordinary term for an official paper that is the basis or proof of certain ideas. As a verb, to document means to explain how a program works and what someone has to do to use it. A program can be documented by means of comments written into the program itself, or by means of a separate, carefully written explanation of what is happening at each stage of the program. There are a lot of different ways to program, and so in any particular case, unless the programmer takes the time to explain what was done and why, it is very hard for another programmer to fix or modify complicated program code. Compared with the challenge of writing the program itself, documenting is hard and boring to do, but it is vital to the success of a program.

documentation The user guides and manuals that explain how to use equipment and programs. Whole new book publishing firms have been created to prepare guides for computers and programs that were sold without adequate documentation of their own.

DOS Stands for Disk Operating System. Pronounce to rhyme with "moss." The DOS is a program that determines how data is to be stored on the **disk** and how it is to be found again. DOS also provides for housekeeping tasks such as removing files that are no longer wanted, **cataloging** the disk to see what is on it, protecting files from accidental erasure, copying files, and keeping track of the different types of files that might be stored together. It is an intimate part of any computer's **operating system**, and each type of computer has its own. Disks of different DOS are not interchangeable.

dot matrix Generally used to describe a popular type of printer that prints by striking a pattern of wires or fine rods within a **matrix** or **array** that might measure five dots by seven, or nine by eleven, or more. Different striking patterns produce different letters and symbols. The more columns and rows in the matrix, the more nearly solid the letters appear. In general, dot matrix printers achieve high speed at fairly low cost, at the expense of **letter-quality** print. But their quality is improving steadily.

double density A technique for storing data on a diskette at twice the normal density. Special diskettes are manufactured for double-density use, but they will also work in single-density applications.

double-sided Intended to be used on both sides. Even **single-sided** disks have magnetic coating on both sides because some drives read from the bottom and some from the top. They are intended to be used on one side only. True double-sided disks are manufactured to be used on both sides simultaneously, since some disk drives have read/write heads positioned to use both sides.

download A personal or home computer can be made to behave like an extension of a large computer located somewhere else. When it is operating under such **terminal software**, it normally is using programs and memory space that belong to the remote computer, and most of its own capabilities are suspended. To download is to arrange for the remote computer to transmit programs or other files down the phone line to the personal computer's disk or internal memory so that they can be used without the remote computer. Stock market information is often downloaded to microcomputers for later analysis, and users of **The Source** and **CompuServe** use downloading to share programs. Downloading can also be used to copy sections of, or even entire, **databases**.

downtime The time when a computer or other piece of equipment is out of order or shut down for maintenance. Downtime is pretty important, because if you expect to do a job with a computer, and the computer is not available, often the job can't be done at all.

dumb terminal A **terminal** that has no provision for doing anything except when attached to a computer, in contrast to **smart terminals**, which can have a wide range of extra capabilities.

dump To dump is to print out everything in a **file**, so that it can be reviewed and corrected, or so that it can be stored away as a **backup** in case of a disk or computer failure. Files can also be dumped from one storage device to another, as from tape to disk or disk to tape.

EBCDIC Stands for Extended Binary Coded Decimal Interchange Code. One of two major codes for representing data in **binary** form. It is pronounced "eb-ceh-dick." The other is known as **ASCII**, pronounced "as-key." Since computers use only numbers, letters must be coded into numbers, and there has to be some agreement on which numbers go with which letters. EBCDIC and ASCII are the two standard coding systems. EBCDIC is most common on large computers, especially IBMs, whereas ASCII is found on most of the smaller and personal computers.

editor An editor is someone who is expert at finding and correcting errors in spelling and grammar. In computers, editors are programs that are used to help write other programs and text, and then find and correct errors in what has been written. A **word processor** consists of an editor to help create the text, and a **formatter** to control line length, indents and other aspects of the way the text will look when printed out. Sometimes the two functions are incorporated into the same program.

electronic mail This term covers all of the various ways you can send messages using computers. The most common form is for the sender of the message to write it into a central computer that the intended receiver also can **access**. The receiver then can read the message and respond in the same way. Each is connected to the central computer by phone lines. Because transmission speeds are very fast, messages can be sent across the country in seconds. Through any phone where you can hook up your **terminal**, you can receive mail quickly or whenever it is convenient. There are many **networks** available for electronic mail, including **The Source** and **CompuServe**, which offer such services to individuals as well as to companies.

enter To type information or program instructions at the keyboard and send them to the computer. Some keyboards use the word ENTER instead of RETURN on the key that corresponds to the carriage return key on an electric typewriter. Usually, the material typed is not actually sent to the computer until that key is pressed.

EPROM Stands for Erasable Programmable Read Only Memory. Most Read Only Memory **(ROM)** is manufactured to contain specific data or programs, and cannot be changed at all. Some ROM is programmable **(PROM)**, meaning that computer users with the right knowledge and equipment can permanently imbed their own programs and data in ROM. Finally, there is a class of ROM, called EPROMs, that can be programmed, erased (with ultraviolet light) and then reprogrammed with something else. You can spot EPROMs because the chips they live in have little windows in their tops, with tape or a label over them. Normal ROM chips are identified by smooth tops with faint printing. Some EPROMs are erased electrically, and they are called EEPROMs, for Electrically Erasable Programmable Read Only Memory.

ERROR A fault, or mistake, in a program or in the data. Also, a message from the computer telling you that it has encountered an error and has stopped the program that was running. A lot of messages from computers are very cryptic and hard to understand, like "ERROR = 3." You are supposed to look up error number 3 in the user guide to find out what happened, but the problem with a lot of user guides is that the explanation is likely to be something like "Range Error—command parameter too large," which is not very useful if you are a beginner. Programs are improving, however. Newer computers have more memory available than the older ones. In other words, more space can be given to meaningful error messages. Program **documentation** is also improving. (See also **error recovery**, below.)

error recovery Programming to allow for human error. Good programs compensate for the fact that people will make mistakes in using them, all the way from answering their prompts incorrectly, to entering wrong or inappropriate data. It's really dreary to go through a long input session with a program, make a little mistake near the end, and then have to go back to the beginning because the program has crashed. Some kinds of mistakes are called "fatal," meaning that the program will stop in its tracks if they are made, forcing you to begin again—they are not fatal in the sense of harming either the program or the computer. Others are called "nonfatal." These can be recovered from if the programmer has anticipated the different ways that the user can go wrong and provided for each of them—for instance, by having the program explain what was expected and ask the question again. Programming with error recovery can convert fatal mistakes into nonfatal ones.

ESCape Most computer keyboards have a key marked ESC. It is one of many nonprinting characters that are used to control the computer; the programmer decides what its specific use will be. Often, the escape key is used to stop a program or to return to a particular part of a program, such as the main **menu** or a set of instructions for the user.

execute To carry out an order already given or to enforce a law already passed. A computer executes instructions that have been written down in the form of a **program**.

expansion slot Many personal and home computers are manufactured with the expectation that users will want to add memory, or any of a variety of special attachments, to make the computer more useful to them. Expansion slots are places inside the computer where such attachments can be made, usually in the form of stiff cards with additional circuits and microchips on them. (See also **Apple**.)

Computer Literacy for Pre-Literates

The school hired me! I couldn't believe that after years of being taught (I was in the 9th grade) I was finally getting a chance to teach. I sat down and tried to think of what I should do first. I would be teaching BASIC to seven- and eight-year-olds so I should make the class fun and informative. Okay, how would a real teacher do it? My teachers always made lists of important words and ideas so I thought that would be a good place to start. I got a pen and wrote down a list of 'COMMANDS,' things like 'RUN' and 'GOTO.' I also put in silly jokes like "What did the computer say to the human? . . . You turn me on!!" When I finished I made copies for all the kids who were going to be in my class. This teaching business wasn't so hard, I thought, as I walked over to the school.

There were ten kids sitting by the computers as I entered the room. I introduced myself, feeling very much like a real teacher. I began the class by explaining all the different parts of the computer. The kids seemed to understand so I started passing out the sheets I had made. As I was distributing them and thinking what a breeze teaching was, I felt a tug on my shirt. I looked down and a little boy waved me closer. He held out the paper and said in a quiet voice, "This is fine but I can't really read too good yet." It was then I decided that being a teacher wasn't going to be so easy after all.

Holding a child's attention can be difficult under any circumstances, and when you start talking flowcharts, variables, and subroutines, it is nearly impossible. Yet these are vital pieces of a programmer's vocabulary and must somehow be communicated to a yelling, fidgeting, gaggle of eight-year-olds. Through trial and error (mostly error) I have come up with a few methods of holding a child's attention, for at least a little while.

Incorporating computer concepts into games is the most effective way to inspire a kid. The games need not be complicated (or even interesting) as long as they involve child-participation and a bit of humor. Perhaps my most successful game was entitled "Shoot E.T. for Fun and Profit" in which a picture of E.T. appeared on the screen and the child would enter the coordinates to make a bullet hole appear at a certain place on E.T.'s body. Sick? Sure, but the kids learned what coordinates were and how to use them.

A particularly good tool for illustrating concepts is the pencil. Never underestimate the power of the directional arrow to show what goes where. Also, whether you are artistically adept, or inept as I am, a sketch can be very useful. Characters such as Mr. Goto and Random the Robot, while being more than a little stupid, do tend to stick in young minds.

If, after you have tried everything else, you still cannot hold a child's attention, I have found boisterous threats of physical violence will sometimes do the trick.

—Colin

feedback A method of controlling a process by measuring its own effect on the environment. A simple example is a household thermostat and heating system. The thermostat responds to a drop in room temperature by turning on the furnace when the temperature reaches a set point on the thermometer. As soon as the temperature rises to another set point, the thermostat turns the furnace off again. The thermometer is providing feedback to the thermostat, which is then telling the furnace what to do. Modern office buildings often use microcomputers to manage heating and air conditioning, using a network of feedback sensors all over the building, inside and out. These sensors measure the effects of sunlight outside and of the heat generated by lights, machinery and people inside, in order to provide only the necessary heat or cooling. Another term for systems that use feedback for control is "cybernetic."

---

fetch To locate an item of data in storage (disk, tape, floppy) and bring it into the main memory for processing. A programmer might refer to "doing a fetch," meaning to get data or a **subroutine** from storage and use it in a program.

---

field Within a **database** file, information is usually arranged so that everything about a certain subject or person in the database is organized as a single **record**. Within the record, the different kinds of information are divided into fields—a separate field each for name, street address, city, state, and zip code, and any other information you might have, such as occupation, date of birth, or hobby. In a news database, there would be separate fields for date, newspaper, edition, author, dateline, subject, location in the paper, length, plus a long field for the text itself, or a summary of the text. With this kind of organization, it is easy to **sort** the records by any field—to make a list of everyone in the file who lives in West Philadelphia, for example, and who is also an astronomer; or to locate articles about West Philadelphia astronomers published during 1980.

file   Like an office file, a computer file is a collection of items of information that have something in common, so that it is convenient to store them together. A file might be as small as a single business letter or as large as a mailing list of many thousands of names and addresses. Programs are written into and stored as files. There are several kinds of files, with different rules about their structure and use. Putting data into a **sequential** or **text file**, for example, is always a matter of adding it on to the end, or replacing something already there. These files grow or shrink like balloons, according to the amount of data in them. **Random binary files**, on the other hand, are of a fixed size, like a box, whether they have anything in them or not. Each has advantages and disadvantages, according to how it is going to be used. (See also **field,** and **record**.)

firmware   Sometimes a program is used so often that the manufacturer writes it onto a special chip called a **PROM** and puts it into the computer so that it is always there when you want it. Since the program lives in a chip, it is like hardware, but because it is still a program, it is software, too. To take both meanings into account, it is called firmware. (See also **EPROM**.)

fixed format   A **file** structure in which all of the **records** must have the same number and type of **fields** and be of the same length. Sometimes fixed format refers to a particular field. For example, a date field can have data in only one format, such as "11-04-84"; "November 4, 1984" would be rejected because it has letters in addition to numbers.

fixed length   A presentation of data, or information, so that every block of data has the same number of items in it, and in the same order. Processing this kind of data is very efficient, because the computer does not have to be told to test each element to make sure that it is the right kind or size. On the other hand, all it takes is one element out of place to turn all of the processing that follows it into garbage.

fixed point A way of representing numbers so that there is no explicit indication of the location of the decimal point; instead, the location of the decimal point is always assumed to be, for instance, two places from the right for dollars-and-cents displays, or all the way to the right for **integer** displays.

flip-flop Describes the basic **binary** switch, a device that is capable of being in either one of only two states—such as on or off, plus or minus, lit or unlit—and which can be signaled to flip from one to the other. Transistors can be flipped from a state of resisting electricity to conducting it, by changing the strength of the current. (See also **semiconductor** and **toggle**.)

floating point A system of representing numbers so that the location of the decimal point can be told by the size of the exponent. For example, a floating-point representation of the number 1234 would be 1.234 X 10^3, and .1234 would be 1.234 X 10^{-1} (also known as "scientific notation"). Computers generally print results in normal decimal notation up to a certain number of decimal places. Beyond that, they revert to floating-point notation because it is a more convenient way to represent very large or very small numbers. Applesoft BASIC, for example, displays nine digits before reverting to scientific notation. In other words, 123456789 prints as 123456789, but 1234567890 prints as 1.23456789E + 10. The "E + 10" means "exponent of + 10."

floppy disk, or diskette Floppy disks are like other computer disks, except that they are smaller, and flexible instead of rigid. They don't really flop like a hound dog's ears—they're more like the cover of this book. They come in three main diameters: 8 inches, 5¼ inches, and 3½ inches. The 8-inch size has been around the longest, and because of its ability to hold large amounts of data, it is still popular with many business computers. The 5¼-inch size is the standard for most personal and home computers, but there are now two new kinds in the 3-inch range, which is about the size of a peanut butter jar lid. What is happening is that the manufacturers are learning how to pack more and more data into smaller and smaller spaces. Floppy disks all have permanent envelopes to protect their surfaces. The envelopes have holes in them for the **heads** to work through, and the disks themselves are never taken out of their envelopes. It is important to keep diskettes clean and free from dust, finger marks, and chocolate milk.

flow chart A flow chart is a map of the way a program will work. Programmers use flow charts to help them figure out the flow of logic and avoid errors. They can be elaborate, with special symbols for every functional step, or quite simple. A board game looks a bit like a flow chart, and it works a bit like one, too. In a board game, the different moves are drawn on the board, and you move toward "home" according to a set of rules, with rolls of the dice determining how far you move in each turn. The board is a map of the game, and it keeps track of where each player is at any time. A flow chart helps the programmer visualize how the action of the program progresses according to its rules.

foreground When a computer is capable of doing more than one thing at a time, the **interactive** part is said to be taking place in foreground. For instance, you might have programmed the computer to calculate a special trajectory to move your spaceship from Earth orbit to Mars orbit with the least amount of energy used. That's a pretty complicated set of calculations, which might take even a computer quite a few minutes, and so you set it up to run in **background**. The computer still has some capacity left over, and so you ask it to play a game of Space Invaders with you in foreground. In large computer systems, background is used for the large jobs that don't need to be completed immediately, and foreground is used for the more urgent work. (See also **batch**.)

format The way data, or information, is arranged. In word processing, it refers to things like line length, paragraphing, pagination, line spacing and footnotes. In a program, format statements define the way the data will look when it is printed out.

form feed A form is a piece of paper. The most common form, of course, is standard typewriter paper, which in the United States measures 8½ x 11 inches. When the computer is printing information out onto continuous paper, or "outputting to the printer," it can simply print line after line from beginning to end, without paying any attention to where one page ends and the next one begins. But the result will be much better looking if it is **formatted**, by having the computer count, say, 54 lines and then skip to the top of the next page, count six more lines, and begin printing on the seventh. The act of skipping to the top of the next page is a form feed, and the top of the page is called **TOF**, for Top Of Form. Of course, forms can be of any length.

FORTRAN Stands for FORmula TRANslation. One of the oldest **high-level languages** for programming computers, FORTRAN was introduced in 1957. There are two standardized versions, FORTRAN-IV and FORTRAN-77, and one or the other is available for nearly every large computer, and for many of the smaller ones as well. It is particularly well suited to **number crunching**, and so it is used for a lot of work in science and economics. (See also **compile.**)

full-duplex Duplex refers to a **MODEM** that can both send and receive data between computers—usually over telephone lines. Full-duplex means it is capable of sending and receiving at the same time. **Half-duplex** means that it can do both, but not at the same time.

function This word has several meanings. It can simply mean some operation like adding or multiplying. Function also defines relationships—travel time is a function of speed and also of distance.

function key A special key on a computer keyboard that can be programmed to do different things, or sometimes to perform a whole series of steps that would otherwise have to be done one at a time.

Adventure Games Are Shared Fantasies

When I sit down to play games on my computer, adventure games are usually the ones I choose. My older brother usually chooses strategy games, which he says are for more "intelligent" people like him, and my younger brother spends his time making his own games. I like adventure games because they are fantasies that several players can share.

Adventure games are those that resemble the famous Dungeons & Dragons game. When that first came out we had the books and the play sheets and the dice all over the house for months. Now all of this is on the computer. It even rolls the dice for you.

I really prefer to play adventure games with friends, but if you have to, you can play by yourself. Because you can save your characters onto a disk, there is a lot less mess around and also less starting over because some piece of paper got lost.

Adventure games revolve around scenarios which are very complicated stories. A lot of information is left out of these stories. You are expected to provide this information, and individual input is what helps make the games exciting. For exam-

ple, you must create your own characters by giving them strength, dexterity, weapons, armor, etc. How well your characters do often depends on how wisely you have equipped them. I found out quickly that a warrior with lots of weapons but no armor or dexterity was asking for trouble.

My favorite game for a long time has been Wizardry (by Sir Tech). We have played this game for over a year and it is still one of the best. My friends and I also play Ultima (by Origin Systems), and Journey to Atlantis (by Synergistic Software).

One of the best features of these adventure games is that the makers are continually updating them. That means that just when you have successfully worked your way through one scenario, the game company comes out with a new one.

Adventure games are made for those who like long-lasting games with fantasy characters. Remember, even though they last a long time, they can be expensive. You might want to share the cost with the friends you play with or, as in my case, with my brothers.

—Jared

garbage Computers have a limited amount of internal memory available, just as we do, and they use disks and other tricks to remember things in the same way we use books. Since the real work takes place in the internal memory, that memory has to be used over and over again. Just as we get our own memories muddled with unwanted data at times—"If only I hadn't said that . . . ."—programs can be muddled by data from a previous run of the same program, called garbage, that is still in memory when the program is run again. The garbage can interfere with the new operation. Good programming practice calls for clearing out such garbage before starting the new calculations—for instance, by setting key locations to equal 0. This process is called "garbage collection."

GET A programming term in some BASICs. It is used to read specific **input** from the keyboard without displaying it. In other systems it can mean to copy some specific data from storage to **RAM**. In that context it is the opposite of **PUT**. You GET data from storage, and PUT data to storage.

GIGO Garbage In, Garbage Out. A lot of people think that computers don't make mistakes, and that is true as long as their programs are properly designed and the data they are fed is accurate, but if you tell the program to divide by 10 when you really mean by 100, the answer will be wrong every time. If the program is helping to calculate batting averages, for example, and you enter 31 times at bat instead of 13, some player is going to be really annoyed at you because you will be understating his average. In other words, if you **input** garbage (bad data) you'll get garbage back. You should learn to look carefully at everything the computer prints out, to make sure that it makes sense.

glitch A glitch is related to a bug. That is, it means that there is something wrong. Bugs are usually found in software and glitches in the computer hardware or the communications lines. Glitches can be extra-frustrating because they often don't happen in a regular pattern, which makes them hard to find and fix.

GOSUB A **subroutine** is a program segment that may be used several times in a program, or even by different programs. GOSUB is the program instruction that sends the action of the program to the subroutine. If the computer has a clock, for example, and you want a program to record the time whenever a call is started and completed through your **MODEM**, you would write the program so that the instructions that deal with checking the clock and recording the time are in a subroutine. Then, each time the program calls for a time-check, you use a GOSUB to send the action to that part of the program. The difference between a GOSUB and a **GOTO** is that a GOTO can be used to skip over sections of a program that are not needed, and GOSUBs always return the action to the line immediately following the GOSUB instruction. (See also **CALL**.)

GOTO A programming instruction that causes the action of the program to jump to another part of the program if a certain set of conditions is met. (IF it is raining, GOTO the section of the program that deals with finger painting rather than with playing out of doors.) If the IF condition is not met, the program ignores the GOTO.

graphics The art, science and programming techniques needed to make pictures on a screen, whether for games, weather forecasting or designing a bathtub or bathyscape.

half-duplex Refers to communications over phone lines between computers, in which the data can flow in only one direction at a time. (See also **full-duplex**.)

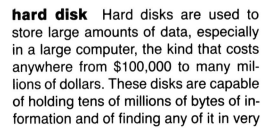

hard disk Hard disks are used to store large amounts of data, especially in a large computer, the kind that costs anywhere from $100,000 to many millions of dollars. These disks are capable of holding tens of millions of bytes of information and of finding any of it in very small fractions of a second. They are often stacked in a disk pack like records in a juke box, each disk with its own read/write **head**. They are extremely expensive, extremely effective and extremely delicate. They have to be handled by experts only, and in special rooms that have no dust in them. The heads travel over the spinning surfaces of the disks so closely that if one were to hit anything as big as a particle of smoke it would cause the surface to be damaged or ruined. If it hit anything as big as a human hair, it would probably destroy the whole disk, and the read/write head as well! (See also **Winchester drive**.)

hard-sectored Information is stored on **disks** according to a pattern, or **format**, laid out by the **operating system**. The available surface of the diskette is divided into **tracks**, and each track is further divided into **sectors**. The **disk drive** can tell which sector is passing the **head** at any time, by reference to a small indexing hole alongside the large, center hole in the diskette. The drive can tell when that hole goes by, and can then figure out the location of every sector on the disk. When sectoring is controlled by a ring of holes around the center, the diskette is said to be hard-sectored. When there is only one small hole, and sectors are further marked magnetically, the diskette is said to be **soft-sectored**.

hardware Everything about the computer that you can touch, including the keyboard, the TV or monitor, the disc drives or cassette player, and all of the little pieces inside that you can perhaps see but shouldn't touch. (See also **software** and **firmware**.)

head The part of the **disk drive** that actually reads information from the disk or diskette surface, or writes information to it. It works very much like the play and record heads on a tape recorder. In drives for microcomputers, the heads actually touch the disks, but in **hard disk** systems, the heads skim along just above the surface, close enough to be damaged by a fingerprint but still not touching the surface. They are sometimes called flying heads. In fact, disk heads have been compared to a very large airplane flying along at an altitude of only 10 feet—about the height of your living room ceiling.

hertz Often abbreviated to Hz, it means cycles per second. Ordinary electrical current in the United States is timed at 60 Hz, and in England at 50 Hz. Some kinds of electrical motors will therefore go ten cycles per second slower in England than in the US. Sound pitch is also measured in hertz. The lowest pipes in a great church organ might rumble at about 20 Hz, while the highest squeak you can hear would be around 20,000 Hz. Those are about the limits of human hearing.

hexadecimal Also called just hex, a numbering system that uses a base of 16. If we had eight fingers on each hand, and had learned to count in units of 16, we might be using hex instead of **decimal**, which is based on units of 10. Using just the numbers 0 through 9 and the six letters A through F, hex can represent any of the 256 possible combinations of **bits** in a **byte** in just two symbols. This economy of space makes hex a nearly universal intermediate language for microcomputers, just one step away from **binary**, and much easier to understand—though still not truly easy.

high-level language When they get right down to it, computers do what they do in **binary** code, which consists of strings of 1's and 0's. In the early days of computing, all of the data and program instructions were laboriously translated into binary and fed into the computers in that form—in their own native language, so to speak. Beginning in the 1950s, computer scientists began to write programs called **compilers** that could read a set of symbols understandable to people—like letters and numbers—and convert them into binary code so that the computers could understand them. **FORTRAN** was the first of these in wide use. Other high-level languages are APL, ALGOL, COBOL, Ada, and Pascal. BASIC, the most common language for micros, is also a high-level language, even though it uses a different kind of translator, called an **interpreter**. This was a very important development because it changed programming from being incredibly difficult to being merely hard, like many other technical jobs. In fact, BASIC was developed specifically to enable people who had no special computer training to write their own programs.

hit In **database** searching, a hit is made every time you find something that meets your **search** criteria. If you were searching a file of newspaper articles for references to ENIAC, a very early computer (1946), and you found 14 references, you would say that you had 14 hits.

host In a computer **network**, the host computer keeps track of the flow of messages and data, and of who is using the network. The host computer would also be responsible for the **log-on** steps by which users enter the system, steering them to the parts they want to use, timing or counting their use of the network's services, and keeping a record for billing purposes.

IBM Stands for International Business Machines, even though the official name of this company is now just IBM. IBM is the biggest company in the computer field, especially in large computers (**mainframes**), but IBM also makes other office equipment such as typewriters and copiers, a popular personal computer, the IBM PC, and the PC Junior.

IF A program instruction used to test whether certain conditions have been met, and then send the action of the program to different parts of the program depending on the results. "IF George weighs more than twice as much as Peter, then add Billy to Peter's team." The instruction to add Billy is a **branch** that is taken only if the weight differences are as great as described. Additional branches might be used to decide whether Billy will add enough weight to Peter's side, or if Joel should be used instead or in addition. (See also **conditional**.)

---

impact printing Traditional typewriters make letters on paper by hitting the paper, through an inked ribbon, with a bit of metal bearing the raised image of the letter chosen. Modern variations on this idea include putting the letters on "daisy wheels," "thimbles," and bouncing "golf balls," but all of these still do their work by smacking the paper with a "formed letter." This is impact printing, and computer printers using it produce **letter-quality** print, similar to the type produced by a good office typewriter, but they are relatively slow and relatively expensive. (See also **dot matrix**.)

---

increment Usually defined as a small portion of something larger, like a slice of ham. In computer terminology it takes on extra meaning as a verb, meaning to add to a number value by a regular amount, usually 1. Counting things is usually a matter of incrementing a **register** by 1 for each of the things you are counting. The "register" can be your fingers, or beads on a string, or the little wheels in a gasoline pump that tell you how much gas is going into your tank. Computers do a lot of incrementing as they keep track of whatever processing they are doing. (See also **decrement**.)

index An index is a list arranged in a certain order, usually alphabetical, that places every item on that list in a particular relationship to all of the others. The index hole in a diskette enables the disk drive to know where every sector on the disk is physically located. (See also **inverted file**.)

infinite loop A kind of program in which the computer is told to do some task, such as adding two numbers together, and then return to the first instruction and do it over again. The computer will go through the **loop** endlessly unless it is stopped by a **break** or by being turned off. Usually an infinite loop is the result of an error in a program that was intended to do the loop a certain number of times, but some infinite loops are useful as such. A digital watch, for example, has a little program that simply counts cycles, so many per second, and then does it again, and again, and again . . . .

initialize Diskettes are usually blank when you buy them, because different computers have different ways of using the space. Initializing organizes the disk so that it can accept and store data sent to it by your particular computer's **DOS**: it copies the DOS onto the diskette and then marks the diskette with magnetic "bookmarks" so that it can later retrieve the information it has stored at the bookmarks. Whenever that disk is **booted**, the DOS is loaded into a special location in the computer's memory, from which it controls all of the computer's storage functions. Once a disk has been initialized for your computer it can be used by any computer of the same type, but usually not by other types.

I/O Stands for INPUT/OUTPUT, and refers generally to the business of getting data and programs into the computer, and results out. A programmer might be heard to say, "I've worked out the processing algorithm. Now all I have to do is the I/O," meaning that the hard part of the program, figuring out how to do the calculations, is finished, and all that remains is the straightforward part having to do with reading data into the program and getting the results out in understandable form.

input Data fed into a computer, or as a verb, to feed information or data into the computer from the keyboard or from some some other device such as a **MODEM** or a disk drive. It really means something that is "put in" to the computer, just as **output** means something that has been "put out" from the computer, whether it's to a printer or to some form of storage. Turning these and other pairs of words around gave them new meaning and also compressed them into less space. This mattered in the early days of computer programming when every byte of memory was precious, and when the normal terminal communicated with the computer at only about ten characters per second. Spelling out more meaningful messages is time-consuming at that speed, and most users were pretty sophisticated, anyway. Similar economies grew out of telegraph and cable practice, in which charges were made by the word, and "downhold" or "update" could get by as one, but "hold down" cost twice as much and "bring up to date" cost four times as much as their abbreviated versions.

instruction A command to the computer to perform some task or operation. A **program** is a series of instructions that have been put together for the computer to **execute** in order. It is useful to think of a program as a stack of familiar punch cards, with one instruction encoded on each card. The cards are fed into the computer in a set order, which is the way most computers used to be programmed and many still are. A lot of programming conventions come from that practice.

integer An integer is a whole number, which is one that does not have a fraction or decimal portion. The number 456 is an integer, but 4.56 is not. Neither is $4\frac{1}{2}$. Numbers with decimal or fractional portions are called "real numbers."

integrated circuit At first, the banks of on/off **binary** switches that make up the heart of a computer were made of electromechanical switches about as big as a fist. Then came vacuum tubes, about as big as a thumb, and hot, which the British call "valves," because they too can alternate between being opened and closed, on or off. Transistors came into general use in the 1950s, using bits of material (**semiconductors**) that could be made to switch back and forth from being conductive to electricity to being resistant to it. Even early transistors were quite small—about half the size of your little finger. Groups of transistors were wired together on circuit boards to make up banks of switches and other components, and computers suddenly got a lot smaller. Then, in the late 1950s, engineers made the leap to making a complete set of parts, all at once, out of the same piece of material, which was the element silicon. Putting several transistors and related parts together on one slice of silicon is called integration. Integration has developed rapidly to the point where many thousands of transistors can be integrated into a small chip that is no bigger than a fingernail paring, with individual transistors too small to see.

Intel   The manufacturer of the first **microprocessor**, the 4004, and the first **EPROM**, in 1971; the first 8-bit microprocessor, the 8008, in 1972, and the first general-purpose microprocessor, the 8080, in 1974. This chip was the heart of the Altair 8800, a kit form of personal microcomputer offered to hobbyists in 1974, and written up in the January 1975 issue of Popular Electronics Magazine. From these events, you can date the microcomputer revolution, which placed real computing power into the hands of ordinary people. Intel continues to be one of the most important manufacturers of **integrated circuits** in the world.

intelligent terminal   There are two kinds of terminals, intelligent and dumb. A **dumb terminal** is one that consists of a keyboard and screen, and just enough circuitry to attach it to a computer and serve as a way of sending instructions and receiving **output**. An intelligent terminal has its own processor and enough memory to enable it to do some processing independent of the computer to which it is normally attached. A store might use an intelligent terminal to collect daily sales data. It would have a program in it that would accept data from the cash registers and store it in a special format until it was time to transmit it to a larger computer for processing overnight.

interactive   Programs that enable you to be in a continuous dialogue with the computer, inputting data and getting results in **real-time**, without having to wait your turn. Arcade games are interactive because the action on the screen corresponds instantly to the action of the **joystick**. Word processors are interactive, of course, and programs that test your arithmetic or language skills are interactive because the computer asks questions and responds to your answers. But programs that can be set up to read whatever data they need from a diskette, do the required processing, and print the results or write them back to the diskette, all without supervision, are said to be **batch** processing programs.

interface   The program or device that controls the way two or more pieces of equipment, or even programs, work together. There is an interface between the computer and the printer, between the computer and the disk drive, and between the computer and the monitor. The keyboard is an interface between us and the computer. Sometimes this word is used to describe purely human interactions, such as the use of an interpreter to enable discussion between people who do not speak the same language, but this use of machine terms to describe human relationships should be avoided because it makes English teachers grind their teeth, and also because it reduces human relationships to mechanical functions.

internal memory The Random Access Memory (**RAM**) that is available to a computer for storing programs and data to be processed. It is usually measured in **kilobytes**, or thousands of bytes, equivalent to thousands of characters. Common sizes for microcomputers are 16K to 64K for 8-bit computers, and 64K to 512K for 16-bit machines, like the IBM PC. There is a strong trend toward more and more internal memory, even in the less expensive machines.

interpreter The **BASIC** language is accompanied in the computer by a program called an interpreter, which you generally are not even aware of. When a program is run, the interpreter is also running. It reads each line of BASIC instruction, converts it into binary machine language and executes it immediately. Most other **high-level languages** use a **compiler** program instead of an interpreter. A compiler reads and translates the whole program before executing any of its instructions. The compiled form of the program can then be saved, in addition to its **source code**. Compilers take up more space in memory than interpreters, and so they tend to be associated with larger machines.

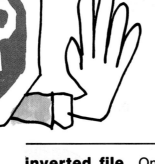

interrupt To stop the **execution** of a program without losing the work done so far. As a noun, it also means the method of interruption. Depending on the kind of interrupt, the action of the program can be jumped to a different section, or on command, the program can resume executing where it left off when the interrupt was issued.

inverted file One of the ways to build a **database** so that it can be searched quickly and efficiently. Database **records** are divided into separate **fields**—one for each kind of information in the database. In an address list database, for example, last name would be one field, street address another, city a third, and so on. An inverted file has an index for each field that is likely to be **searched**. Each index is a list of the contents of its field for each record in the file, plus a code that says where on the disk each record can be found. Therefore, instead of searching the whole file for "Smith," the program searches only the last name index for Smith, and makes a list of the locations of all of the Smiths in the file. The second stage of the search might look at the first name index to find all of the "Amandas" in the file, and the third stage would be to compare the list of all Smiths with the list of all Amandas, and select only those records that occur in both lists, that is, people who have the last name, "Smith," and the first name, "Amanda." The fields that are indexed are often called **keys**.

iterate Means to do something again, or to repeat. (The more familiar form of the word, used in conversation, is "reiterate," meaning to review something already said.) In computer terminology, iterate describes the action of a **loop**, which is repeating a set of instructions a certain number of times, or until some condition is met. Adding to 100 by 2's requires 50 iterations.

The Superiority of Ten-Fingered Typing
And Other Hints on Getting Along With Your Computer

As a former two-fingered typist, I feel I can say with some authority that two-fingered typing is incredibly inferior to the ten-fingered method. With the ten-fingered method, each finger is assigned to certain keys, and it knows (with practice) where those keys are. When you type with this method, you have the computer or type-writer keyboard just about memorized, and you don't have to spend so much time searching for letters. When you get to be good at typing, it becomes almost automatic, so you don't have to think about where the letters are, or how to type; your fingers take care of that. You have only to think about what you want to say.

The ten-fingered method also makes composing on the computer or typewriter turn out better. If you are struggling to find letters all the time, it is harder to put across what you want to say smoothly, and it is easy for you to unconsciously omit certain things, or make your sentences abrupt and empty, just because it is such a labor to type out the words.

In the end, all of these things add up to support the standard ten-fingered typing system for people who use computers.

Here are some other hints which will help you to enjoy your computer.

Do not put your computer in such a position that when you sit at the keyboard, you can look over the monitor out the window, because if you then raise your eyes, they have to adjust to the brighter light outside. When you look back at the screen, they have to adjust again. All this adjusting can make your eyes tired, and when you're tired, you make more mistakes. (Take that little piece of advice from me: I know from experience!) Also, try not to have a bright light behind you, because it will reflect off the monitor screen, which can also make your eyes tired.

Another thing: Never have food or drink near the computer. Believe me, sticky orange juice in the disk drive or Coke between the keys is a disaster. And I bet you'd be pretty disgusted to find potato chip grease stains on the computer paper.

One more word from the wise: If you're going to be working for a long time (for instance, if you're writing a computer dictionary!), make yourself comfortable. Get a nice chair, maybe with a pillow, so you won't fidget and lose your concentration.

—Amanda

JCL (Job Control Language)

Fortunately, JCL is not something that most beginners have to contend with, but since the term crops up from time to time, it is useful to know what it means. In **interactive** computing the program asks a series of questions, and the information it needs is typed in at the keyboard. If the same program were to be run in **batch** mode, without human supervision, those same questions would still have to be answered, and in the same order. Those answers, in fact, control the processing job that is to be done. JCL is a particular way of telling batch-type programs what they are supposed to do, and it has been in use longer than interactive programs. It happens to be a very picky, difficult and unforgiving language, with few built-in safeguards. JCL experts are a special breed of programmer, like karate black belts or microsurgeons, but those skills are being superseded by more **user-friendly** control programs.

joystick

Attached by a cable to the computer, the joystick is a little box with a small lever sticking out of the top, and a couple of buttons on the side. The joystick controls movement in many action games; buttons fire the guns or lasers. Joysticks are also used to draw figures on the screen in graphics programs. The term comes from aviation. The steering column of early aircraft was called a joystick. Pulling it back toward the pilot caused the plane to climb; pushing it forward made it dive; and side-to-side movement controlled turns. Similarly, a computer joystick lever can be tilted in any direction, and its movement is translated into the movement of the **cursor** on the screen of your **monitor** or TV. Side-to-side movement causes the cursor to move from side to side along the **x-axis**, while up-and-down movement moves the cursor up and down on the screen (along the **y-axis**).

justification   To align text so that all of the lines begin and/or end at the same place on the page. Left justification, with a "ragged right" (uneven) margin, is the usual format for typewritten text. Right justification involves making the right margin line up as well. Typesetters and more sophisticated word processors align both margins by inserting partial spaces between letters. Less-sophisticated word processors justify by inserting whole spaces between words.

key   A word or sequence of letters that can be used to encode and decode data, just as a key opens and closes a lock. In another sense, key refers to certain words in a **database** that can be most quickly found. Finally, to key means to enter data at the keyboard, also known as "keyboarding" or "keystroking."

keypad   In addition to the usual letter and number/symbol keys found on a typewriter, a computer terminal often has an extra set of keys on one side, called a keypad, or numeric keypad. These keys are laid out like the keys on a calculator, labeled with numbers, and can be used instead of the numbers on the top row of the keyboard. If you are more used to calculators than to typewriters, this keypad can speed up the process of entering a lot of numeric data. The keys of the keypad can be programmed as special **function keys** when they are not being used for numeric data entry.

keypunch   To prepare data for entry into a computer by typing it on a machine that punches holes in computer **cards** in patterns that correspond to the numbers and letters. For many years, this was the best way to enter data; and it is still in wide use, especially when it is desirable to have a physical, as well as a magnetic, image of each **record**. Cards can be printed as they are punched, so that they are both human- and machine-readable.

keyword   A **field** in a **database** that can be used to locate quickly the **record** it is a part of. Keywords are indexed to be found in a few seconds, no matter how large the file. (See also **inverted file**.)

kilo-   Prefix meaning one thousand. A kilogram is 1,000 grams and a kilometer is 1,000 meters. (But see **kilobyte**, below.)

kilobyte (Kb or Kbyte) A little more than 1,000 **bytes**—1,024, to be exact. The most basic unit of computer memory is that two-position switch called a **bit**, or binary digit. A byte usually has eight bits. Other important sizes for bytes, or **words**, are 16 and 32 bits. The number 1,024 is evenly divisible by 2, 8, 16, and 32. It is also 2^{10} (2 times itself ten times). A "kilo" of 1,024 parts is therefore a convenient way to measure memory. For example, 64Kb translates to 64 X 1,024 = 65,536 bytes.

kludge A kludge is a badly designed, badly made piece of hardware, or a patch (a hasty afterthought) in a program. A kludge will probably cause problems later on because it was not carefully thought out.

What Parents Should Know About Computer Camps

Most people, especially adults, have the wrong idea about computer camp. Parents think that their kids are going to be locked up in a room all day with a computer, getting eyestrain and no sun or sports like in a regular camp. Kids sometimes have the wrong idea, too. They think they are going to play games like blasting the aliens all day. It's not like that at all, at least not in the camp I went to in Connecticut.

Computer camp is a specialty camp like a baseball, tennis, or riding camp. Instead of riding a horse for four hours a day, two in the morning and two in the afternoon, you have instruction in computers. At the beginning of camp you sign up for a computer language. This could be BASIC, Pascal, LOGO, assembly language, or others. Also, you can learn how to use special software packages like VisiCalc, Bank Street Writer, or others. At my camp, there were also lessons in how to take a computer apart and how to care for the equipment. This was my second year at this camp and I went for a month. Last year, I went for two weeks. Both years I had a really great time.

Most of the counselors were college students—math or computer science majors. Some were real computer freaks still in their teens but a lot were older than the counselors in regular camps.

In the evenings, the counselors would take turns talking or teaching about something that they or the kids were interested in.

One counselor who had created and sold some programs gave a lecture on how to write a game, and all of the things you have to do to get it sold.

My camp locked up the computer rooms after the lessons. This was good, because a lot of us would have stayed there all day. The camp had about 35 Apple IIe computers, 40 Texas Instruments computers and six or seven IBM's, but each of us had our favorite machine to work on. A couple of us discovered that the back

door of the computer room opened into the bathroom, and that by waiting there, we could get into the computer room first and get the machines we wanted, no matter how many kids there were lined up outside waiting for the main doors to be unlocked. When we were not working, we did all of the usual camp stuff, like swimming, basketball, soccer, baseball, Ping-Pong, arts and crafts, ultimate Frisbee, etc.

At the end of each two-week session, there was a project due in the language you had learned. Most beginners took LOGO and BASIC. This year I took Beginning and Advanced Assembly. I enjoyed it, even though it was hard and I need a lot more practice before I'm really good at it.

The best thing about computer camp is always having someone around who will answer all the questions you have when you are trying to learn about computers. Also, I made some new friends. We can write to each other on our computers, and even talk to each other or leave electronic messages for each other through our MODEMs.

A lot of kids think they want to own computers, but this is a big expense for families. Many parents think computers are only an expensive toy that the kids will play with for a week and then it will sit in a corner gathering dust. Most of the kids in my bunkhouse who were there for the first time had come to learn about computers and to prove to their parents that this was not a toy or just a game machine. They hoped that when they went home from camp, their families were going to purchase a computer. I don't know any kid who went home not still wanting one.

I don't know why there aren't any more girls at camp. There were about eight boys for every girl. Maybe the boys get interested sooner because of the games with missiles and tanks. All I know is that when you get to programming, all you need is a good mind.

—Ian

label   A name given to a **file**, a **rec-ord**, or even an item of data. It could be a single letter or a group of letters that don't spell any normal word.

LCD   Stands for Liquid Crystal Display. Many digital watches and instrument displays use LCDs, since they are lightweight and require so little power. Some very portable personal computers now use LCDs instead of TV-like monitors, and there will be more of them in the future. LCDs are usually dark gray against a light gray background.

LED   Stands for Light Emitting Diode. Used for watches and instrument displays, LEDs are small, usually red, lights, although they can be any color. They require more power than LCDs, but they can also be read in the dark.

letter quality   There are many different ways of printing out the results of work done on a computer. **Dot matrix** printing is the cheapest and fastest method available to most personal and home computer users. Letter quality printing looks as if it were done on an office typewriter, and many letter quality printers are adapted from office type-writers. The range of speeds available is from 12 characters per second (cps) to 30 cps. In a letter quality printer, speed is expensive. The price range is similar to the speed range: the fastest ones are more than twice as expensive as the slowest. (See also **impact print-ing**.)

library   In a public library, there are many books on open shelves, constantly available for anyone to use. Similarly, in a large computer system, there is a library of programs that are con-stantly available for any user to **run**, and files that any user can **access**. This library of open programs is separate from private files that individual users may maintain on the same system.

line feed On a manual typewriter, a "carriage return" is a lever that moves the roller holding the paper back to the right at the end of each line, so that the left-hand side of the paper can be typed on. It also cranks the paper up one line to make room for a new typed line; that movement is called line feed. Many electric typewriters move the print head back and forth, instead of the carriage, but the effect is the same. With computers, a line feed is normally associated with a **return** or an **enter** command, but it is really a separate function. Some printers supply line feeds automatically, so it is important when you are hooking up a printer to know which is going to supply the line feeds: the printer or the computer? If both are, the result will be double spacing rather than the expected single spacing. If neither is, then all of the lines will be printed on top of each other, which is an economical use of paper, but not very practical otherwise.

line printer This is a very high speed printer that uses a different print head for each print position across the paper. If the printer can print 132 columns of numbers, it has 132 print positions, usually ten to the inch. A line of print is sent from the computer to the printer, and it is printed all at once, like high kicks in a chorus line. The quality of type of these **impact printers** is often not very good; the generally poor quality has contributed to giving the word **printout** a bad name. But at speeds of over one thousand lines per minute, there are times when a poor quality of type is acceptable, such as when you need a readable copy of something for **backup** purposes but you don't ever intend actually to read it.

LIST A computer command to print out the coded instructions that make up a **program**. If entered alone, "LIST" will tell the computer to print out whatever program is in its current memory. If followed by a program name, "LIST" will cause that program to be **loaded** from the disk and then displayed or printed. Almost any BASIC program can be listed, as can the **source code** (but not the **compiled** versions) of other languages. A **printout** of a program is often called a program listing.

LOAD A computer command to get a program file from disk or other storage, and load it into current memory so that it can be **LISTed** or copied, or **compiled**, or edited, or **RUN**.

logical operator A great deal of programming is bound up with defining a set of conditions and determining whether they have been met, before proceeding to the next step, as in the following example: "IF A is greater than B AND A is less than C AND A is NOT equal to D, then ring the bell." The words AND, OR, and NOT are logical operators in the system of symbolic logic used by computers and based on the work of the English mathematician George Boole in the middle of the last century. They are also called "**Boolean operators.**"

LOGO The name of a programming language developed by Seymour Papert, especially for teaching young children how computers work and how to program them. LOGO uses a system called Turtle Graphics to show how lines and curves can be drawn on the screen by giving specific instructions to the turtle. Those instructions can then be combined into programs that make complex pictures.

log-on The process of dialing up a remote computer system, such as **The Source** or **CompuServe**, and entering your account number for billing purposes, and your **password** to assure the computer that you are authorized to use that account.

loop A loop is a series of program steps that are repeated a number of times. An **infinite loop** is one that goes 'round and 'round, indefinitely. An infinite loop might be set up to test the temperature outside, report it on a special screen, and loop back to test it again, repeating that sequence until told to stop. A more common kind of loop begins with the word "for," as in "for as many pages as there are in this book, count the words on each page and add that number to the previous total." The loop would be repeated until there were no more pages, and the total would be the word count of the book.

LSI Stands for Large Scale Integration, the process of packing many thousands of transistors and other components onto a single, small chip of silicon. (See also **integrated circuit** and **Intel**.)

Games of Strategy and Manipulation

As far as I'm concerned, strategy games are the only ones for a "thinking man." If you like chess and involved board games, then the strategy games available for the computer are for you.

My current favorite is North Atlantic '86 (by Strategic Simulations). It is based on a hypothetical take-over of the North Atlantic by Soviet Block forces in the year 1986. I have been playing this game for almost a year and find it remains stimulating and even compelling. I play either alone or with friends and I can take either the Soviet or the NATO side. Through the game I have become familiar with current weaponry (classes of ships, planes, and missiles) and possible strategies of the superpowers. It is not surprising that military institutions often engage in just this kind of game-playing.

Strategic games do not have to involve armed conflict. I also enjoy games like Cartels and Cutthroats (also by SSI) where you design and run your own corporation in the world of high finance. In this game you even have quarterly reports which you can print out.

For sports enthusiasts, games like Computer Quarterback or Baseball involve the strategy of picking teams and running plays. My idea of a sports game, however, is Galactic Gladiator, a sort of a futuristic Roman contest. (All three are also by Strategic Simulations.)

Actually, what I'm saying is that strategy games are good over a long period of time. You can play for 26 hours straight, or leave for a month and the game is still there waiting for you. While others may pale, I can see myself playing strategy games into adulthood, even some day with my own children.

—Colin

machine-independent There are so many different kinds of computers, and so many different ways of programming them, that programs that will work on one usually will not work on another kind. Programs that will work on only one kind of machine are said to be machine-specific. Programs that will work on several different kinds are said to be "machine-independent."

machine language, machine code The native language of computers is **binary** code, but there are certain sets of binary codes that each computer uses to pass instructions back and forth among its different parts. These sets are called machine language. **Assembly language**, in turn, is designed so that each of its statements corresponds to a particular machine language instruction. Machine code and assembly language are not for beginners, but it is not uncommon to find a fairly simple BASIC program that includes or requires some machine code or assembly language.

macro If **micro-** means very small, macro- means very large and complex. In computers, a macro is usually a single instruction that can stand for a whole group, especially in **assembly language**. In word processing, a macro is usually a single word or letter code that stands for several. If you were writing a story about James James Morrison Morrison Weatherby George Dupree, for example, and if you always referred to him in full, as James James Morrison Morrison Weatherby George Dupree, as A.A. Milne did in his poem, you might assign a code like "%" to James James Morrison Morrison Weatherby George Dupree, so that every time you type a "%," you would get instead, "James James Morrison Morrison Weatherby George Dupree." That "%" would be a macro.

magnetic memory Data is stored on **disks** and **tape** in the same way music or television programs are recorded on tape. In both cases, a thin plastic film is coated with a thin layer of an oxide of iron—chemically similar to plain old rust. The write/record head of the drive is a sensitive electromagnet, whose magnetic field rapidly changes with the data that is being fed into it. As the magnetic field changes, the head leaves a track of magnetized particles in the film. When the read head passes over these tracks, its field is affected by the fields of the particles, and the data or music can be accurately read or played. The little particles of iron will retain their magnetic tracks for periods of up to several years, but can also be reused, for new data, over and over again.

mainframe A general term for any large computer—not a micro or a mini. The term probably comes from the practice of building computers on a series of circuit boards kept in place by a metal frame that holds them by their edges and provides a rigid support.

main memory Usually refers to the internal memory of computers, where all the data and programs are stored while they are being used or processed. **RAM** is main memory. So is **core**, in older machines, with both types being constantly reused. **ROM**, where certain programs are stored permanently, can also be considered part of the main memory. Main memory is also called "primary memory"; disks are called secondary memory, or secondary storage. In **mainframe** computers this term refers to a special portion of the internal memory that has faster **access** times that the rest.

mass storage **Disk** or **tape** drive, or drives, used to store programs and data when the computer is turned off or working on something else.

matrix A display of information laid out in columns and rows, like multiplication tables or a table of distances between cities, in which you can find one city across the top row, the other down the left-hand hand column, and the distance between them at the intersection of that column and row. The important thing about matrices is that each intersection can be easily referred to, or **addressed**, by the labels of its column and row. For instance, B12 would be a simple and convenient way to refer to the data in Column B, Row 12. **Dot matrix** printing is accomplished by specifying the columns and rows of the dots that make up each letter.

mega- Prefix meaning one million (1,000,000); for example, megabyte— often shortened to just "meg"—means one million bytes. Mega- is also used informally to mean any very large amount, as in "megadose," which means a very large dose of something.

menu Just as a restaurant menu is a list of choices of things to eat, a program menu is a way of showing the user what choices are available in a piece of software. Some programs make practically every move a matter of selecting from a list of choices, so that the user has to know very little about the program to be able to use it. Such programs are sometimes described as being "menu-driven," in contrast to programs that require the user to remember or look up the range of options available at different points in the program. Menu-driven programs are easier to learn, but generally slower to use than non-menu-driven programs. Some have menus for beginners to use and also a way for experts to bypass them.

micro- Prefix meaning one millionth (10^{-6}), or in a more general sense, just meaning very small, as in microchip or microcomputer. It's important to keep in mind that "very small" is a relative term. For example, geologists have recently discovered in the Pacific Ocean a previously unsuspected separate tectonic plate, one of the slowly shifting pieces of the earth's crust. They are describing it as a "microplate" because it measures "only" 200 square miles.

microcode Coded instruction for the operation of the microprocessor, usually built in by the manufacturer and not changeable. This program is so fundamental to each microprocessor that it is practically part of the hardware.

microcomputer A computer system consisting of a **microprocessor** chip and the related **integrated circuits** needed to control memory and **I/O**.

microprocessor The **central processing unit** of a microcomputer. It is usually a single integrated circuit on a chip of silicon, with several thousand transistors and related parts. If you start with a microprocessor, add memory chips (**RAM** and **ROM**); chips to perform arithmetic and logic functions; chips to control the flow of data between the different parts; a keyboard and monitor to talk to it with; and a way to store data, then you have a **microcomputer**.

milli- A prefix meaning one thousandth (10^{-3}). A millimeter is one thousandth of a meter, a milligram is one thousandth of a gram, and a millipede is a small bug with a whole lot of legs.

mnemonic   Pronounced as if it did not have the first "m," this word means "assisting the memory." The little tune young children learn with their ABCs is mnemonic, as are many rhymes—"a pint's a pound the world around"; "i before e, except after c." There are a lot of mnemonic tricks used in programs, to help you remember what to do—for example, "D" is for delete; "I" is for insert; "T" is for top of file; "B" is for bottom of file, etc., all depending on what the programmer thought was mnemonic.

model   An imitation by the computer of some real-life situation or process. A model can help the user to study and understand a set of circumstances, or to forecast what will happen if some of those circumstances are changed. A farmer might make a model of chicken raising. He knows how long it takes to raise a chicken from the egg to the market, and he knows the current prices of feed and other things he has to buy to raise that chicken to a certain weight. His model might help him figure out what will happen to his chicken business if the price of feed goes up by a certain amount. Or he might use the model to find out whether it would be profitable to send the chickens to market a little earlier, getting less but saving on feed. This kind of model can work pretty well because the farmer understands the relationships between the various parts of the chicken business. An inexperienced farmer using such a model should be able to make decisions that are as good as those of an experienced one, other things being equal (which they are not). Whole industries, even national economies, can be modeled like this, but the models become unreliable because understanding how all of the parts fit together and affect each other becomes much more difficult as the models increase in size. Nevertheless, modeling is a major application for computers, large and small.

MODEM   Stands for MOdulate/ DEModulate. A device that is attached in between the telephone and the computer so that you can use your computer to "talk" over phone lines to other computers that have MODEMs attached to them. The MODEMs simply process the computer's signal so that it can be sent accurately over the telephone lines (modulate), and then reverse the process at the other end (demodulate), so the receiving computer can understand it. In this way, computers can share data, send and receive messages, and even play games with someone across the country (if the owners feel like paying long distance charges). See also **acoustic coupler, the Source**, and **CompuServe**.)

module　A module is a unit of either hardware or software, generally one that can be used, or at least tested, by itself, but which is intended to function as a part of a system. Modular hardware is designed so that if something goes wrong with part of it, one or two modules can easily be replaced and the overall system can get back into service quickly. Modular software is written so that each stage of the program can be written, tested and **debugged** separately, even by different programmers. It is often written so that the modules can be used in different programs without modification. (See also **subroutine**.)

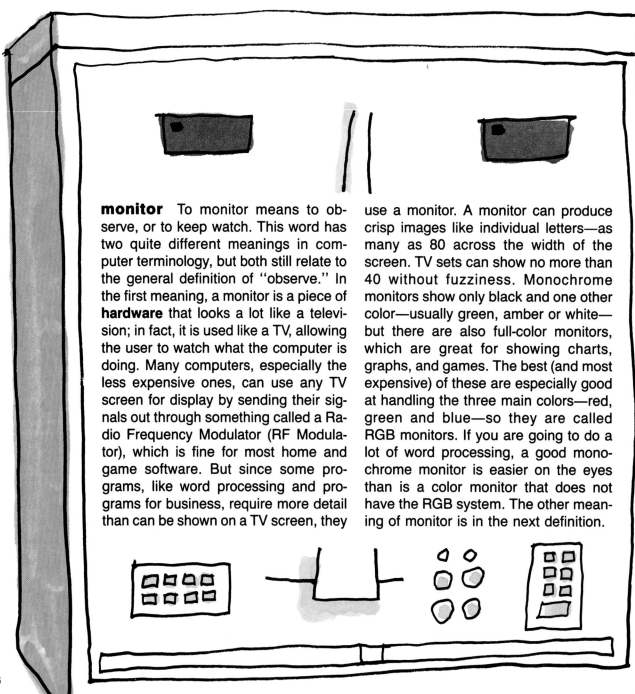

monitor　To monitor means to observe, or to keep watch. This word has two quite different meanings in computer terminology, but both still relate to the general definition of "observe." In the first meaning, a monitor is a piece of **hardware** that looks a lot like a television; in fact, it is used like a TV, allowing the user to watch what the computer is doing. Many computers, especially the less expensive ones, can use any TV screen for display by sending their signals out through something called a Radio Frequency Modulator (RF Modulator), which is fine for most home and game software. But since some programs, like word processing and programs for business, require more detail than can be shown on a TV screen, they use a monitor. A monitor can produce crisp images like individual letters—as many as 80 across the width of the screen. TV sets can show no more than 40 without fuzziness. Monochrome monitors show only black and one other color—usually green, amber or white—but there are also full-color monitors, which are great for showing charts, graphs, and games. The best (and most expensive) of these are especially good at handling the three main colors—red, green and blue—so they are called RGB monitors. If you are going to do a lot of word processing, a good monochrome monitor is easier on the eyes than is a color monitor that does not have the RGB system. The other meaning of monitor is in the next definition.

monitor program In its other meaning, monitor is a piece of **software** that is actually the heart of the **operating system** that every computer must have. The monitor program keeps constant watch on the status of the keyboard, for example, and relays each keystroke to the computer. It knows both that **peripheral** equipment is attached to the computer, and what its status is. The monitor program supervises everything else that is going on in the computer. Most microcomputer users are not even aware of the monitor program, but it is always there; and advanced programmers can use many of its special capabilities to enhance their programs.

MOS Stands for Metal Oxide Semiconductor, one of the techniques for making large scale integrated circuits. (See **LSI** and **VLSI**.)

most significant digit The leftmost digit in a number. In the number 3475, for example, "3" is the most significant digit. If you had that many gallons of water in a tank, you could think of it as 3000 gallons plus 400 gallons plus 70 gallons plus five gallons. The most significant amount in the breakdown is the 3000 gallons.

motherboard All of the chips and other components of computers and of most other electronic devices are attached to special plastic boards. These boards have been printed with lines of metal that make up the circuits connecting them all together. There might be one or several such boards in a computer, but the motherboard is the one that contains the microprocessor itself; all the others are attached to it and controlled by it.

mouse Apple's computer, the Lisa, has made this term popular, and has also encouraged other manufacturers to offer similar devices. A mouse is a gadget about the size of a bar of soap, and it is attached to the computer by a thin cable. It has little wheels or a ball on its flat side, and one or two buttons on the top. As you roll it around on a flat surface, the wheels pick up the direction and distance traveled, and the **cur**sor moves on the screen in the same way. The mouse substitutes for the arrow keys on the keyboard. If you had a **menu** of choices on the screen, for instance, the mouse could be used to move the cursor to the one you want, and pressing a button would send the appropriate signal to begin that section of the program. The idea is to reduce the need for a lot of typing.

MP/M Stands for Multiprogramming-control Program for Microcomputers. It is an **operating system** intended for use by computers that are capable of managing more than one user and/or more than program at the same time. It was developed by Digital Research Corporation, the same company that markets **CP/M**, which is one of the most widely used operating systems for microcomputers.

multiprocessor A computer capable of running more than one program at the same time, for the same or different users.

nano- A prefix meaning one thousand millionth (10^{-9}), or one billionth. This term is normally used in talking about very fast computer memories, in which access times are measured in nanoseconds.

natural language Natural languages are the ones we speak and write—English, Spanish, Chinese, etc.—which developed over hundreds of years. They all have rules of grammar and syntax, some of them pretty strict, but they are not necessarily efficient when it comes to writing clear instructions that can be interpreted in only one way. For computers, special languages such as **BASIC, FORTRAN** and **CO-BOL** were developed. These **high-level languages** bridge the gap between natural language and unambiguous instructions that a computer can understand.

nested loop In programming, a term for a **loop** inside another loop. Loops control repetitive actions, in which the computer is told to perform the same series of steps over and over again until some condition is met, such as reading the first 20 names from a file and printing each on the screen long enough for human eyes to read it. In this case, the main loop would be the instructions to get each name and to print it to the screen. But computers go so fast that we would not be able to read the names. The answer is to insert a delay loop inside the main loop. That way, after each name is printed on the screen, the computer enters the inside loop, which tells it to count to 1000 and then return to the main loop, which tells it to get another name. Counting to 1000 will take a few seconds, long enough for us to read the name. (To provide the right amount of time, that number might have to be 500 or 10,000, depending on the computer.)

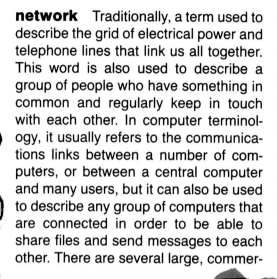

network Traditionally, a term used to describe the grid of electrical power and telephone lines that link us all together. This word is also used to describe a group of people who have something in common and regularly keep in touch with each other. In computer terminology, it usually refers to the communications links between a number of computers, or between a central computer and many users, but it can also be used to describe any group of computers that are connected in order to be able to share files and send messages to each other. There are several large, commercial services that offer networking facilities via phone lines, such as **Tymnet** and **Telenet**, and others such as General Electric Information Services Company that maintain networks in support of their **timesharing** services. Many large companies have their private networks, but it is also possible to set up a network among microcomputers in a small business or a school. Networks of friends, colleagues and associates have sprung up across the country via the computer networks—an interesting merging of the old and new meanings of the word.

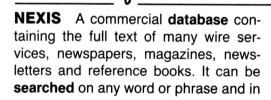

NEXIS A commercial **database** containing the full text of many wire services, newspapers, magazines, newsletters and reference books. It can be **searched** on any word or phrase and in just a few seconds it will find the articles that the search terms appear in. It is a powerful research tool, but expensive to use and not available through most personal computer and MODEM hookups.

n-key rollover Also known as "type-ahead," this term means that even if you can type faster than the computer or typewriter can put the letters on screen or paper, the letters will not be lost. The codes for the letters that you type go first into a **buffer** and then to the screen or paper. They can pile up in the buffer until you slow down enough for the letters on the screen to catch up. The "n" refers to the size of the buffer, in **bytes**. (See also **QWERTY**.)

nonprinting character A **control character** that is visible on the screen but that does not print out onto paper. These characters are used to pass instructions to the computer and to the printer, usually to describe the **format**—that is, to tell the printer exactly how the text should look on the page.

nonvolatile Volatile means change-able or transitory. Nonvolatile means permanent. These terms are used to describe different kinds of memory. Read-only memory **(ROM)**, is nonvolatile because once it is programmed a certain way, it will stay that way, whether the computer is on or off. Random access memory **(RAM)** is called volatile because new information can always be written over whatever is already there, and everything in it is lost when the power is turned off.

number crunching Slang term for computing. It usually refers to programs that do a lot of numerical or statistical computations.

My Cross Country Treasure Hunt—With CB

I was fooling around with our Apple the other night. My object was to do a graphics dump. A graphics dump is a printout of a picture you have created in the computer and have displayed on the screen. The manuals I had didn't seem to have the information I needed, and I was really getting desperate. Then I thought of using CompuServe, which we had started using a few weeks earlier. CompuServe is a monster computer somewhere in the western hemisphere, I'm not sure where. After 6 pm and on weekends, it lets us little guys, like Apples, IBMs, Commodores, TRS-80s, and Ataris talk to each other and play games on it for only about $5 or $6 per hour.

So I called CompuServe, using a device called a MODEM hooked in between our Apple and the phone, and after I got logged on with David Smith's ID Number and password, I went to a service called CB. CompuServe has a lot of services such as news, shopping services, electronic mail, weather reports and airline schedules, but I like CB the best. It's sort of like CB radio, where people all over the county can

talk to each other through the keyboard, no matter what kind of computer they have.

CB is really terrific. Even my mom likes it. (My dad doesn't use a computer.) I explained my problem with the graphics dump and then typed, "Apple help wanted." Everyone on CB was ready to help. First I talked to a man in Seattle who owns a bookstore. He was friendly, but also new at this, so he couldn't help much. But we had a nice talk anyway.

Finally someone suggested that I try the Apple Special Interest Group (SIG) part of the system. Among the Apple specialists, I found someone who knew the answers and was even ready to download some software to my disk.

This was how I finally got the answer, but it was really like a treasure hunt that took me all over the country, and it was a lot of fun. Also, while I was getting my answer, I thought up a lot more questions. It's nice to know that there are a lot of people out there who will help me with the answers, and David was real nice about the bill.

—Ian

object code Program instructions in a form that the computer can act on directly. Programs written in a **high-level language** like **FORTRAN** are called **source code**, which has to be translated into object code by a **compiler** before the computer can understand it. The compiler translates the source code into object code, which can then be stored in memory in that form. Object code is very efficient because it has to be compiled only once. But to change it, you have to go back and edit the source code, then recompile. Object code is in **binary** form.

octal A numbering system using 8 as a base, instead of the 10 of **decimal**, or the 16 of **hexadecimal** (hex). Octal has been pretty much superseded by hex, which is more convenient for 8-bit machines (most micros).

off-line Not hooked up to a computer. In a place where much information is available **on-line** from computer files, information that is not available that way is said to be off-line. Also, when you want to use information that is available on-line, it is sometimes handier and cheaper to use the computer to identify the information you want and to enter an order for it to be printed and mailed to you. This is called an off-line print.

on-line Being attached to or available via a computer hookup. When you are working at the computer or at a terminal attached to a computer by phone lines, you can say you are on-line. Some newspapers have all of their back issues in computer files that can be **searched** for news items about any topic. These files are said to be on-line. Public databases that can be **accessed** through a computer or terminal hookup are on-line.

OPEN It is useful to think of computer files as having many of the same characteristics as traditional file folders stored in a file cabinet. The disk or diskette can be thought of as the cabinet, and the individual files as Manila folders or envelopes. Just as with file folders, computer files have to be opened before anything can be read from them, or added to them, or deleted from them. And they have to be **CLOSEd** before they can be put aside for other work to be done. Computer programs have to allow for opening and closing files, and for keeping track of which ones are being used at all times.

operating system (OS) The program that converts a collection of microchips into a computer. Every computer has one, and some can use several different ones, although not at the same time. The operating system is a program that is always running, down in the lower depths of the computer. It knows the status of each **peripheral**, and hears the stroke of every key. When you type "RUN" at the keyboard, for instance, the operating system interprets your request to begin a program, and knows that you mean the one currently in memory if you do not mention a specific name. OS also takes care of the computer's housekeeping chores, such as storing and deleting files on your disks. Since Apple computers were initially developed to be used without a disk drive, Apple's operating system is imbedded in the computer, in ROM, and its disk operating system **(DOS)** is **booted** from a diskette. Most other personal computers boot the whole operating system from a diskette. The most widely used operating system for microcomputers is called CP/M, (Control Program for Microcomputers), developed by Digital Research. Other popular systems are MS/DOS, developed by Microsoft, and PC/DOS, developed for the IBM Personal Computer. Programs written on machines using a particular OS can often be run on other brands of machines that use the same OS—but not often enough so that you can assume it. Always ask.

output Anything that a program sends or transmits from the computer's memory or from devices under its control, such as disk drives. Data sent to the screen so that you can read it is output. Anything printed is output. For the sending computer, data transmitted through a **MODEM** to another computer is output, but of course, the receiving device considers it **input**. The difference between input and output is sometimes not clear, but it helps if you keep in mind that it's a program that is doing the work, and as far as the program is concerned, anything it asks for is input to it, and anything it sends or prints is output from it.

overwrite To write over, usually in the sense of writing new information on top of old in memory, and erasing the old data in the process. In word processing, you usually have a choice of ways to make a correction. One is to insert new material next to the old and then delete the old, and the other is to overwrite the old.

P

packet switching A way of transmitting data among computers. In a **network** the flow of data among the various units needs to be regulated so that it is both efficient and secure. The network itself might consist of one central unit with many satellite computers sharing data under its supervision, or it might consist of several clusters of machines connected at more than one point, so that data could flow along more than one path between any two points. Packet switching is a method of breaking the flow of data into small sets, or packets, each of which includes a copy of its destination address. Each packet can then take the best route to that destination, independent of all the rest. The program controlling the network puts the packets back together in the right order at the destination.

---

paper tape An old-fashioned method of storing programs and data, paper tape was developed for Teletype machines, which transmitted at 10 characters per second—faster than most typists can type accurately, but slow by computer standards. Paper tape is about an inch wide. The Teletype has an attachment that punches holes in coded patterns, including guide holes that keep the tape from slipping. Messages can be prepared in advance of transmission, and then sent at the most efficient speed, for accuracy and to save money. This device was easy to adapt for preparing programs for the early computers, as an alternative to punched cards. Some Teletype machines still use paper tape, but not many computers do any more because it is slow and fairly clumsy. The true ancestor of paper tape is ticker tape, which was developed in the nineteenth century to record output from a telegraph line, usually for stock market quotations. There is not much ticker tape in a ticker tape parade these days—now it's mostly punched cards that flutter down from the high windows of Wall Street.

parallel Refers to several things happening at the same time, as in parallel transmission or parallel processing. The most common use of the term is to describe a method of transmission between computer and printer. Parallel communications take place along a bundle of wires, a separate wire for each **bit** in a **byte** being sent: each byte marches from computer to printer along eight separate wires, the eight bits arriving at the same time, just like a column of soldiers marching eight abreast. The alternative method is called **serial** communication. It uses one pair of wires, or a **coaxial cable,** and the bits proceed one after another, like soldiers walking in single file. In processing, most computers work sequentially—that is, one step after another, from beginning to end. Addition of six numbers is done in five stages: first by adding the first pair together, then adding that result to the third number, and that to the fourth, and so on, until there are no more numbers to add. The last sum is the answer. Some advanced computers can break a problem like that down into just two stages, adding three pairs in three different processors at the same time, and then adding those results together for the answer. This parallel processing is potentially much faster than serial processing, but more complex, and much research on it is being done in **artificial intelligence** laboratories. (See also **Von Neumann machine**.)

parameter Parameter comes from a Greek word meaning "measure." Sometimes we use this word to mean limits or boundaries, as in the parameters of a task or problem. In math, a parameter is a known value in an equation, which is to say that parameters are the parts you know or can measure in order to solve a problem. If you are solving $A \times B = 32$, and "A" is given as 4, then that 4 is a parameter. To print out text from your word processor, you give the computer a set of parameters that define line length, margins, page length, pagination, spacing, etc. Most of these can be preset as **defaults** so that you don't have to worry about them each time you print.

parity One way to make sure that data being sent over a phone line is not garbled by noise or other problems with the line is to add together the ones and zeros of each **byte's** first seven **bits** as they are transmitted; and then set the remaining bit equal to one or zero in order to make the sum of the eight bits always even or always odd. This is permissible because only the first seven are used for data, anyway. If the number is to be even, parity is said to be even; if odd, then parity is odd. If the receiving computer knows what parity is being used, it can do a parity check by adding the bits as they come through. If it gets an odd number when it is expecting an even, it knows that an error has occurred and can mark the file or take some other action. Of course, if more than one bit in a byte is switched, the errors may cancel each other out and be invisible to a parity check; but since errors rarely occur so neatly as two in a byte, some of the bad data in the transmission will likely be caught by a parity check, and that should make the whole transmission suspect.

Pascal A programming language named after the seventeenth-century French mathematician Blaise Pascal. Pascal lends itself well to **structured programming**, in which the elements of the problem to be solved are broken down (decomposed) into units that are small enough to be programmed and tested independently. That makes it easier to test and track down **bugs**. Pascal **compiles** into a form of **machine language** called pseudocode, or p-code, which has the unique property of being highly portable between different kinds of computers. It is a more powerful language than BASIC, but not much more complicated to learn, and it is destined to become one of the most important languages for microcomputers.

password A password is a word or mixture of letters and numbers that is supposed to be known only to the program and a particular user or set of users. If the program recognizes the password given, it then gives that user **access** to private files, checking accounts, or systems that charge fees for computer resources used. If you use systems that are protected by passwords, you should be careful about who knows yours, and change it frequently.

PEEK A programming command in BASIC that is used to examine the contents of particular locations, or **addresses,** in the computer's memory. For example, on the Apple II, a "PEEK -16336" will sound a soft click because the switch for that click is located at memory address -16336. If you program a dozen PEEKS to that location (FOR I = 1 TO 12 : PRINT PEEK (-16336) : NEXT I) you will hear a series of clicks like a faint drum roll. This PEEK is used for sound effects in a lot of programs.

peripheral Peripheral means "at the edge." A computer peripheral is any device that is attached to the computer, such as a printer, plotter, disk drive, MODEM, or keyboard.

permanent storage With computers, permanence becomes a relative term. Stone tablets, though not very convenient, make permanent records. In computer terms, permanent storage usually means data stored on a magnetic **disk, diskette**, or **tape**, in contrast to data held in the kind of temporary or volatile memory (**RAM**) that goes away whenever the power is turned off. The permanence of these magnetic media is relative because disk and tape are good for only about two years without significant loss, if they are carefully stored away from stray magnetic fields. Punched cards and punched tape are more secure yet, except from moisture; and an occasional printout of all programs and data onto paper is a fine backup.

pico- A prefix meaning one trillionth, or a million millionth, or 10^{-12}. It is not very often used in in general conversation, but is helpful when talking about super computers that are performing millions of operations per second.

pilot A programming language developed especially for teachers to use in preparing computer-aided instruction materials. Pilot is called an "authoring language" because it simplifies the process of preparing a program that can be used to teach kids. It does not require programming skill, or even knowledge of a programming language.

pirate A pirate is a thief, someone who copies copyrighted programs and sells or gives them away. There is a great deal of software available that is in the public domain—owned by everybody because the authors either forgot to copyright, or decided simply to give the programs to the world. Anyone can make unlimited copies of those programs, and give or sell them to anyone without being a pirate. But if the author of an original program, whether it is a game or a business program, has registered it under the copyright laws, the author's rights to sell and profit from the sale of the program are protected by law. It is a law that is difficult to enforce in most cases, however. When you have bought a copyrighted program, making copies for your own use and for **backup** purposes is acceptable; but making extra copies for someone else, even to give away, is a kind of theft from the author whose time and skill made the program possible, and whose money has been invested in packaging, advertising and supporting it. The copyright law was written a long time ago to encourage the exchange of ideas and information by giving authors the right to profit from their work. Authors receive nothing for pirated copies, and if pirates are unrestrained, there will be fewer good programs.

pixel Think of your **monitor** or TV screen as a grid, with many horizontal and vertical lines. The little boxes that are formed by the intersecting lines are called pixels. (The four lines you draw for tic-tac-toe make a grid with nine pixels.) The more lines there are on the screen, the more pixels there are and the smaller each one is. Each pixel can be individually turned on and off, or given a color. The more pixels there are, the sharper the lines that can be shown on the screen. Apple's low-resolution (not very sharp) graphics have 40 vertical columns and 48 horizontal rows, for a total of 1920 pixels, but the high-resolution graphics screen has 192 by 280, or 53,760 pixels. The IBM PC has optional graphics with 200 by 320, or 64,000 pixels, and a high-resolution mode with 200 by 640 (128,000 pixels).

plot To draw a diagram on the computer screen, to make a graph of some information that is usually in the form of numbers, or to draw lines between points on the screen. All computer graphics are really variations on plotting, since the location of every dot of color, or **pixel**, is is determined by reference to its coordinates on the screen. (See also **x-axis**.)

POKE A programming command that puts a piece of information into a specific pigeonhole, or **address**, in the computer's memory. In the Apple II, memory location 32 records the value for the left-hand margin of the screen. "POKE 32,6" sets the left margin to 6, where it remains until "POKE 32,0" sets it back to the extreme left, its normal position.

port A place where an accessory or **peripheral** device such as a printer, monitor or MODEM can be plugged in. The two main types are called **serial** and **parallel** ports, and the standard serial port is called an **RS-232C**. Most personal and home computers have or can have at least one of each. The parallel port is usually used for a printer, and the serial port for a printer or a **MODEM**.

precedence The order in which mathematical things happen. An expression like "3 + 6 X 2" can be solved to equal either 18 or 15, depending on whether you do the addition first, or the multiplication. In this case, 15 is the right answer, because the normal rules of precedence call for multiplication and division to be done before addition and subtraction, which must then be carried out from left to right. The best way to avoid confusion is to use a parenthesis, since precedence calls for expressions inside parentheses always to be solved first: (3 + 6) X 2 = 18, or 3 + (6 X 2) = 15. The term comes from the language of diplomacy, in which the rank or social standing of the different people at a gathering determines the order in which they can speak or where they will sit at dinner.

primary key In a **database**, it is wasteful and confusing to have duplicate **records**, or records that are about different things but are hard to tell apart. That is why we have a bank account number, and a social security number, and a license plate number—to keep all of us Smiths from getting mixed up with one another and with the rest of the world. That number is a primary key, intended to make its record different from all of the rest. A database has an index of such primary keys, and each key has attached to it an address where its full record can be found on the disk. By searching the index, the program can very quickly find any record. Indices of secondary **keys** can also be made, to speed the process of finding records when you don't know the primary key. In a complex database system, there might be a secondary key index for every **field** in the record. The primary key does not always have to be a number, but numbers are most convenient for this purpose.

printout Simply a printed copy of a computer file. It might be a letter to grandmother printed out of a word processing program, or the result of some computation, or a print copy of a program's **source code**, which is also called a program listing.

program A list of instructions, written in a language that the computer can understand or interpret into something that it can understand. BASIC, FORTRAN, ALGOL, Pascal, APL, Ada, and COBOL are all **high-level languages** that have been developed for writing programs. Programming is called **software** to distinguish it from the mechanical and electronic parts called **hardware**. A computer is a combination of software and hardware, programs and machinery. Neither can be used without the other.

PROM Stands for Programmable Read Only Memory. It's just like ROM, except that the manufacturing process is different. With the right equipment, sophisticated microprocessor owners can insert their own programs into PROMs, add these PROMs to their computers, and then run those programs from the PROMs instead of from disk. This is one of the ways in which computers are customized for special tasks. Once programmed, the contents of PROMs are fixed permanently, but there is a class of PROM called **EPROM**, that can be erased and reprogrammed.

protocol A protocol is a record of a meeting, especially a diplomatic one. It is also a code of diplomatic and military etiquette—the rules of conduct—and it is in this sense that the word has been adapted in computer jargon to mean the rules for using a certain computer or computer program. Diplomatic and military protocol is very strict and detailed, and computer protocols are, too, especially the older ones written at a time when there was less memory available for "user-friendly" features.

PUT A programming term (in FOR-TRAN), meaning to send an item of information to the disk for storage. Its counterpart command is "**GET**", for retrieving data from storage.

From Pac-Man to PIE Writer:
Game Player Discovers Word Processing

We have had a computer for three years. My dad uses it to write (mostly about computers) and to do budgets for my school and some businesses he is involved with, and my mother works on it, too. At first I used it mostly for games. I beat my dad pretty regularly at Pac-Man, Space Invaders, Sneakers, and just about any other game we get. (He says that's because I spend more time playing than he does, but actually it is because I have better reflexes.)

But now the thing I really like best is the word processor program. (We use PIE Writer, by Hayden Software.) I took a short course in typing at school last year, and now I use the computer to do all of my longer papers and my biology notes. But I haven't exactly given up games.

My eighth-grade senior project last year came to about 20 pages, and my faculty adviser put me through three different drafts. I made my notes longhand, as usual, but I wrote the whole first draft on the computer. After that was done, it was fairly easy to reorganize it, add some extra material in the middle and make grammatical and spelling corrections. Then, just push a few buttons and the computer kindly prints out a fresh copy, with none of the grief of retyping all of it. I got a good grade, and some of it had to be because I could keep making revisions until I got it the way I wanted it, right up to the last minute.

But all is not perfect. Sometimes the computer overheats or something and just stops. Then whatever is in there is just lost. That's the kind of thing that makes you very careful about saving your work into a disk file every page or so. That way, you will never lose too much.

And one time, I turned in a paper that was missing a key paragraph. Somehow, it got dropped out between the draft and the final version. I don't trust the thing as much as I used to—I know how important it is to check my work—but I would sure hate to have to do without it. It was some trouble to learn, but worth it.

—Amanda

queue A queue (pronounced "cue") is a waiting line, as in front of the movie theater. When several jobs are waiting to be run on a computer, they are said to be "in the queue."

QWERTY The first six letters on a standard typewriter keyboard. Early typewriters were likely to jam if the typist went too fast, and so a keyboard was designed to actually slow the typist down by placing a lot of frequently needed letters in awkward places. That QWERTY layout became the standard, and we still use it, even though modern typewriters don't jam when the keys are pressed too fast. Some computer keyboards can be programmed to use different and more efficient arrangements of keys, but everyone is still being taught the QWERTY keyboard, and so it is difficult to change.

RAM Stands for Random Access Memory. The main memory banks of a computer are composed of RAM, and computers are usually classified acording to how much RAM they have. (See also **random access** and **random binary file**) An important thing about RAM is that it is stable only as long as the computer is turned on. Actually, there are two kinds—static and dynamic. The static kind stays the way it is until you change it or until power is turned off. Dynamic RAM must be constantly refreshed, many times per second, or it decays into a state of forgetful randomness. As soon as the power is turned off, both kinds of RAM forget everything, instantly and completely. Any information that you want to save must be copied onto a disk or cassette, or printed on paper. RAM, then, is where the computer keeps instructions and data that it needs currently for whatever task you have assigned to it. The next task might use the same memory areas over again, simply writing new information over the old. RAM memory is said to be volatile, or easily changed.

random access Random means that things are scattered without any particular order or pattern. In computers, random access also means that although a particular item of information might be located anywhere in the computer's memory, there is a way of keeping track of each individual byte, so that any part of memory can be addressed directly. This is more efficient than keeping information in a list. If I want to locate Roger in a RAM memory, I don't have to read about Randolph or Rebecca or Richard or Robert first, much less Alfred, Betty, Cathy, David . . . Quasimodo first. (" . . . " is a way of saying, "and all of those in between.")

random binary file A type of file structure that can be read from or written to without reference to any other part of the file. Random in this case does not mean "by chance." It means that each part of the file can be accessed by its **address**. Using such random access files is much faster, on the average, than using **sequential files**, which have to be read from the beginning, but random access files have the disadvantage of having to be set up at a specified size in advance. Sequential files can be added to as long as memory lasts.

random number A number selected by chance, so that a series of such numbers would have no pattern, and the next number in the series would be unpredictable. Computer languages have a random number generator built into them, to enable a programmer easily to call for a random number in a program. Random numbers are used to roll dice and pick cards and choose paths in computer games, to make them unpredictable. A program intended to teach geography might quiz you by asking a series of questions. The computer's random number generator could be used to make sure that you get a different set of questions each time you take a quiz. True randomness, the kind that can meet all of the mathematical and statistical tests, is quite hard to arrange, and so most microcomputers make do with "pseudo random" numbers—adequate for games and most other applications, but not perfectly random.

read To get data or a program from storage and put it into the computer's **internal memory** for use or for further processing. You "read" a file or "read" the disk. It is the opposite of **write**.

read-only Describes a kind of computer memory that cannot be altered. A disk that has had its **write-protect** notch covered is a kind of read-only memory that is temporary. **ROM** and **PROM** are permanent read-only memories, and **EPROM** is somewhere in between.

real-time Describes processing that takes place right away, as opposed to processing that might be put into a **queue** and processed in **batch** form. Most personal and home computer applications are real-time programs. If airline reservation systems are to be effective, they must operate in real-time, since reservation clerks and travel agents need to know seat availability from minute to minute.

record In a **database**, a record is a collection of information about a single subject. Databases are usually designed so that each record is the same size, with the information on each subject organized into separate **fields**, each field containing only one kind of information. For example, in a baseball card database, the data on each player would make a separate record. Each record would have separate fields for name, team, position, RBI, home runs, lifetime batting average, year started, other teams played on, etc. Given this structure, the program can **sort** the records by any field or combination of fields, for example, to find all catchers whose lifetime batting average is greater than .325.

refresh Some kinds of memory (dynamic **RAM**) tend to decay into forgetfulness and must be constantly reminded of what they are supposed to remember. In this sense only, they are a bit like rabbits. Refreshing is the process of sending the data to this kind of memory over and over again, many times per second.

register A special, high-speed memory location used for storing intermediate results. A computer totals a column of numbers by adding the first two numbers, then adding the result to the next number, and so on until it runs out of numbers to add. The results of each successive addition have to be stored, in the same way you would jot down on scrap paper subtotals in a complicated calculation. The sole function of the scrap paper is to keep track of where you are, at any point on the way to the answer. A register performs the same function in a somewhat more formal manner. A computer may have many

separate registers, but most have only a few, which are used over and over again. The size of each register is usually the same as a computer **word**.

remote access Being able to use a computer from a distance, usually through a **MODEM** and telephone lines. Generally refers to the **timesharing** use of large computers, but it is possible to access a personal computer from any remote location, if its MODEM has the ability to answer the phone automatically and the computer has been left on, with appropriate **software** running. With special attachments, it is even possible to turn the computer on and off from a remote location. (See also **bulletin board**.)

reserved word In programming languages, certain words have special meanings, and therefore cannot be used as **variable** names or as **program** names. Examples are RUN, IF, GOTO, AND, DATA, END, CALL, FOR and SAVE. BASIC has about 100 such words.

response time The time it takes for a computer to respond to **input** from the keyboard. In **timesharing** situations, where the computer might be serving many users at the same time, the response time will increase as the number of users increases. It is amazing how irritating a delay of a few seconds can be, even when it is associated with a task that used to take hours and now is taking only minutes. Timesharing utilities such as General Electric Information Services Company are very sensitive to response times, and adjust their prices to encourage users to do only high priority work during peak usage hours, and lower priority work at times when there are fewer users on the system, or overnight. Their problems are very much like those of an electric utility, which must have enough power available to run air conditioners and subways during rush hours and then have expensive equipment idle at other times.

restore Normally when you **delete** a file, it is gone for good. But because of the way files are stored on the disk, it is sometimes possible to restore them. Part of the disk is devoted to maintaining a directory of all of the files on the disk, and details of where they are. Deletion simply erases the entry in the directory and frees up the space that the file used. As long as you don't use that space for anything else, you should be able to get the deleted file back, using special **utility** software usually available from a dealer.

return On an older typewriter, once a line has been typed, a carriage return lever positions the paper to begin a new line. Teletype machines evolved from typewriters, and computer terminals evolved from Teletypes, and so now a return command signals the end of a line (or the end of an instruction) even when there is no paper to be carried back and forth. Return has another use. The terminal is always "listening" to the keyboard, and storing what it hears in a temporary memory called a **buffer**. With some programs, the computer responds to certain keystrokes immediately, but in most situations, the instruction or data is not even sent to the computer until the return key is pressed. On some keyboards, the word ENTER has been substituted for RETURN, to make its function clearer.

reverse video   Also called inverse video, this is a way of highlighting letters or words by reversing the background and foreground colors, for example, to show dark lettering against a light background, instead of light lettering against a dark background. In systems whose displays are limited to all upper case letters, reverse video is often used to denote capitals.

ribbon cable   A type of cable used for connections between different parts of a computer system, such as between the keyboard and the **CPU** or between the CPU and the **disk drive** or printer. It is made up of a set of eight more insulated wires that are bonded together into a flat strip like a ribbon. Sometimes the individual wires are colorcoded to help the person who makes the connections to keep them straight. In computers, ribbon cables are usually limited in length from a few inches to a few feet.

right justify   A term from word processing and typesetting that means to align the right margin. Most microcomputer word processors do this by padding out short lines with spaces. The more sophisticated programs can pad by inserting partial spaces between letters, which is useful only if you have a sophisticated printer as well. Text that is not right justified is called "ragged right."

ROM   Stands for Read Only Memory. Most computer memory is arranged so that you can write information into it and also read that information back from it. ROM is a kind of memory that is used for information that never changes: you can read what's there, but you can't write anything new into it. For example, the binary meanings of each keystroke are usually imbedded in ROM, so that whenever you turn on the computer and type a certain letter on the keyboard, that letter will always appear on the screen. The meanings of many of the routine commands that the computer uses over and over again are also found in the ROM area. Different manufacturers have different ideas on the ways in which their products will be used, and so they all use ROM differently. Apple puts Applesoft, its version of the BASIC language, into ROM, so that it is always there. Others require you to load the language from a disk each time you want to use it, on the theory that you might want to use one of several other versions of BASIC, or some other language entirely. ROM is said to be "nonvolatile," which means that it is difficult or impossible to change. Unlike **RAM**, it does not disappear when you turn the computer off. In your own memory, ROM would be like the kind of memory you use to store your name and the other details that make you a unique personality. RAM would be where you store an unfamiliar phone number just long enough to dial it, and then forget it.

RS-232C A standard for connecting computers to various **peripheral** devices, such as printers and **MODEMs**. RS-232C is a **serial**-type interface, and when you are told that a certain device has an RS-232C **port**, it means that you should be able to plug it right into any other device with the same kind of port—assuming that the two things are intended to work together in the first place.

RUN The usual command for telling a **program** to start **executing** its instructions. A program that is under way is said to be running.

In Defense of Two-fingered Typing

I'm a two-fingered typist and I'm pretty fast that way. When I was twelve I took a typing elective in school but when it came to the computer, the keyboard was a little different. Since I was already looking around for the punctuation keys, I found that the two-fingered method was faster for me. So far, this has worked out. Most of my papers for school are not that long, or if they are long, I am able to break them up into short sections and store them on a disk. Now I have started high school and I can see I might have a problem in the future with long papers that need footnotes. I tried one of the typing tutor programs but it was boring. Maybe someone will write a good typing program for kids my age soon. In the meantime, here is one ten-fingered method you might want to try. How it works is you call your mom and see if she will type while you dictate.

—Jared

P.S. to Jared: I feel sorry for anyone who can't do a long paper without calling his mother!—Amanda.

S-100 bus   Probably the oldest computer **bus** for which there is a formal standard, and therefore widely used. A bus is a circuit that links all of the parts of the computer together, and enables them to pass.

---

scratch file   A temporary computer **file** that serves the same purpose as scratch paper, i.e., a place to write down intermediate results, but in a form in which they can be used in further calculations. The file can be whatever size and type that is needed. Generally, a scratch file is deleted after the program run has been completed, but it is sometimes saved for future reference. Scratch files saved beyond their immediate uses can clutter up your disks.

---

search   To look for data in a file, usually a database, in which the object is to find all of the **records** that meet certain criteria. An automobile dealer with a customer database might want to locate all buyers of a particular model car for a

recall. Or he might have just bought a used Corvette on a trade-in, and want to find everyone who had asked for a used sports cars in the last few months. The process of finding them in the database is called a search.

search term   In the previous definition, the car model, dates, Corvette, etc., are search terms. Some database systems are searchable only by certain terms; others are capable of being searched by any word or phrase that occurs in them. In such a full-text database, search terms are any words you choose to search by, in order to find articles on the subject you are interested in. For instance, if you wanted to know the name of the political party that Walter Mondale and Hubert Humphrey both belonged to in Minnesota, you would search by "Minnesota and party and Humphrey and Mondale," and you would be rewarded with just those articles that included all four terms. One of them would surely mention the Farmer's Democratic Party.

sector   Information is stored on **disks** and **diskettes** according to a very particular pattern. The details of the pattern vary from system to system, but the general outline is the same. Disks are divided into concentric circles like rings on a target, called **tracks**, and the tracks are further divided into sectors, or segments, around the tracks. A sector is the smallest individually addressable segment on the disk, and although a single **file** might be scattered across many different sectors, no sector can hold parts of more than one file. The Apple II's **disk operating system** uses 35 tracks of 16 sectors each, each sector holding 256 bytes, for a maximum disk capacity of 35 X 16 X 256 = 143,360 bytes. Three tracks are reserved for DOS itself, and one more for a directory of the disk, leaving 31 X 16 = 496 sectors or 126,976 bytes of usable storage, but it is unusual to fill every sector to the brim, and so in actual practice the capacity will be somewhat less.

seek time   The time it takes to move the read or write **head** of a **disk drive** to a particular **track** on the disk. Seek time is measured in small fractions of a second. When the application requires frequent access to the disk, to read or write information, seek time can have a major bearing on the overall **response time** of a system.

semiconductor   A material that can both conduct electricity and resist it, depending on the voltage. Below a certain level, say 5 volts, the material does not conduct any electricity at all. Over that threshold, the "juice" flows freely. Semiconducting materials like silicon and germanium are the basis of **transistors**, which make up the basic on-off switches of **binary** computer memory.

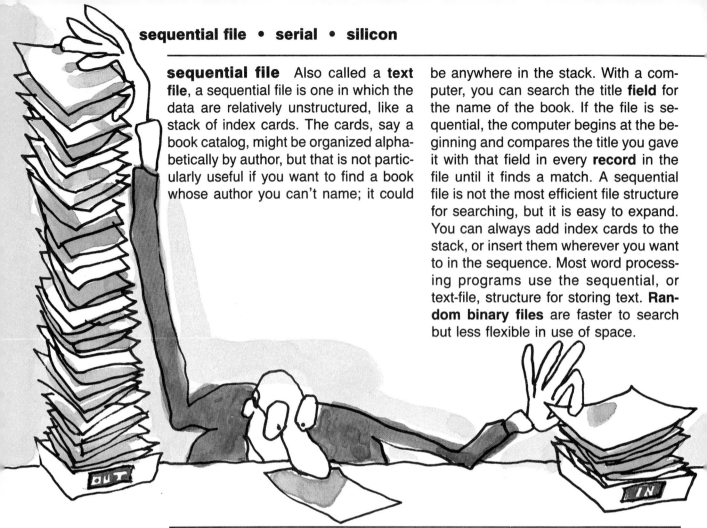

sequential file   Also called a **text file**, a sequential file is one in which the data are relatively unstructured, like a stack of index cards. The cards, say a book catalog, might be organized alphabetically by author, but that is not particularly useful if you want to find a book whose author you can't name; it could be anywhere in the stack. With a computer, you can search the title **field** for the name of the book. If the file is sequential, the computer begins at the beginning and compares the title you gave it with that field in every **record** in the file until it finds a match. A sequential file is not the most efficient file structure for searching, but it is easy to expand. You can always add index cards to the stack, or insert them wherever you want to in the sequence. Most word processing programs use the sequential, or text-file, structure for storing text. **Random binary files** are faster to search but less flexible in use of space.

serial   Any set of things arranged in a row, one after another, are in a series, or in serial form. A magazine "serial" is a story or article that is published in a series of installments. In computers, serial generally refers to the way in which data are transferred from one part to another internally, or to a printer or **MODEM**. Serial transmission uses one pair of wires, and the data are transmitted one bit at a time, with a **stop bit** inserted at regular intervals (agreed upon by both sender and receiver) to keep things synchronized. Serial transmission is good for some applications, **parallel** transmission for others. Serial is slower but more reliable over distances greater than a few feet. (See also **RS-232C**.)

silicon   Next to oxygen, silicon is the most abundant element in the earth's crust. Semiconductors are made from refined beach sand, which is mostly silicon, melted and transformed into giant crystals. These are then sawed into thin wafers, imprinted with the hundreds of copies of the diagrams needed to make **integrated circuits**, and then cut up into the tiny individual chips that go into computers and other devices. Pure silicon is a good insulator (glass is silicon) and its ability to act as a semiconductor is created by selectively imbedding in it (which is called "doping") small amounts of other elements, such as arsenic, phosphorus and boron. The process is not simple, but we are lucky that the raw material, at least, is cheap and plentiful.

simulation A simulation is a model of a real-life situation. It can be a game, or a historical situation, or a model of a business problem. The model is a **program** that asks the same questions you would be faced with in real life, and responds to your answers in a way that is realistic in terms of that situation. If the model is a good one, it can help you figure out what the results of a particular action might be. Businesses use models to try to figure out the effect of changing prices or manufacturing methods, or to predict the effects of changes in the rate of inflation. There are many simulation games, like Wizardry and Haunted House, which feature mazes that you must negotiate with the help of fellow seekers and junk that you pick up along the way. If you choose the wrong companions or pick up too much, you can't move fast enough; if you decline to carry the rope, shovel, log, etc., you might not be able to get across the ravine before the baddies get you. In another kind of simulation, you can replay great battles of the past, taking the part of one side and having the computer take the other. You can be Napoleon and try to win at Waterloo by using your forces differently, or Churchill fighting the Battle of Britain.

single-sided Describes a diskette that is intended to be used on only one side. Most diskettes have magnetic coating on both sides because some disk drives read from the bottom and some from the top. Some people use both sides by cutting an extra write-permit notch in the side opposite the existing one in the diskette's jacket. This is not recommended, because writing on one side might harm the material on the other. (See also **double-sided**.)

slave Any device that is used only under the control of another, or that mimics another. Normally, you use either a monitor or a printer to receive information from the computer, but you might want to use both, for instance, to make an exact record of a session in which you used your computer as a terminal to "talk" to someone through a **timesharing** service like **CompuServe**. The printer would then be slaved to the monitor.

smart terminal A **terminal** that is capable of doing some processing of its own, independent of the computer to which it is normally attached. It has at least some local memory, and a microprocessor of its own, usually intended for temporary data storage and editing. Entering data into the terminal's memory and editing it there will reduce the amount of **on-line** time needed to load that data into the computer.

Softcard   An expansion card for the Apple II computer, it contains a Z-80 microprocessor chip and enables the Apple to run programs written for the Z-80, especially the popular **CP/M Operating System**, and much of the software written for it.

soft-sectored   **Initializing** a diskette prepares it for use by your particular **disk operating system**, by establishing on it the pattern of **tracks** and **sectors** that will be used to store your data. Some systems use diskettes that have the sector pattern already established on them. They are described as **hard-sectored**. Diskettes used by systems that impose the sectoring pattern as part of initialization are soft-sectored. Soft-sectored disks have a single small hole in the disk material next to the large hole in the center. This can be seen through a window in the jacket. Hard-sectored disks have a series of holes in the disk, one for each sector. Hard- and soft-sectored diskettes are not interchangeable.

software   Computers have to be told what to do, in very detailed sets of instructions called programs. Programs are software. Software can also refer to the data that computers process, but generally it means programs. Programs imbedded in memory chips (**ROM, PROM, EPROM**) are called **firmware**, and all of the parts you can see and feel are called **hardware**.

sort   To arrange or rearrange items in a list, alphabetically, numerically or by some other criterion. It also means to arrange **records** in a **database** according to the contents of a particular **field**. One sort might be by date, another by size, another by value and still another by zip code.

source code   Computer instructions (**programs**) written in any of the high-level languages, like **FORTRAN, COBOL, APL** or **BASIC**. Source code can be fairly easily read by programmers. Once translated into language the computer can act on, it is called **object code**, and is readable only by rare experts (and computers).

Source, The   One of two computer timesharing, networking and information utilities especially designed for use by microcomputer owners, the other being **CompuServe**. Via The Source or CompuServe, the personal or home computer user with a **MODEM** can tap into hundreds of databases, shop for discounted merchandise, read sports, news and stock market quotes, play strategy games against other people who might be using the system at the same time, exchange information with others, take part in discussions on topics of general interest, or join in a Special Interest Group (SIG) to exchange information about a particular kind of micro, nuclear disarmament or Chinese cooking. The Source and CompuServe are both used to store private messages, addressed by code, and readable only by the addressee whenever he or she signs on to the system. In this way, micros of different kinds can exchange messages that might not otherwise be compatible.

spool Most micros can do only one thing at a time, which means that when yours is printing something out, it can do nothing else, and neither can you. If the printout is long and the printer is slow, you may be out of business for a good while. To spool is to send the material to be printed to another device, often a memory **buffer**, from which it can be printed while you are doing something else with the main machine. The transfer of data from your main memory to the spooler can be very fast.

standards A standard is simply an agreed-upon way of doing things. **RS-232C** is a standard for communications. **S-100** is a standard **bus** for microcomputers. F77 is a standard version of FORTRAN, which means that any program written in F77 should run on any computer with an F77 **compiler**, without modification. There is no such standard for **BASIC**.

static Noise on a communications line, and by extension, any irritating noise like "Clean up your room before dinner!" or "Have you done your homework?"

static RAM, static memory Memory that holds whatever has been entered into it as long as the power is on, as opposed to dynamic **RAM** or memory, which requires constant **refreshing** to maintain its contents.

stop bit In **asynchronous serial** transmission of data, an extra **bit** is inserted at specific intervals, such as at every eighth bit, i.e., at the end of each **byte**. Since seven bits are all that are needed to encode any character in **binary**, the eighth bit in a byte can be used to keep the sending and receiving computers in sync, and to provide a means of testing for data integrity through its **parity** (whether the sum of the bits in a byte is odd or even). This sort of thing is usually handled by the communications software, and the most you will be expected to do is agree on where the stop bits are supposed to fall, and whether the parity is odd or even, and answer the prompts accordingly. A start bit is an extra bit used to signal the beginning of an asynchronous serial transmission.

storage Collectively, the various methods of storing data in computer memories of all kinds: **RAM, disk,** magnetic **tape, cards, paper tape**, etc.

Is It True that Educational Games Can be Fun?

There are some games that are supposed to be fun and at the same time teach you something. This is a good idea but I think it has a long way to go. Knowing what is fun for kids to do—not just one time but repeatedly—is not easy. Schools like this kind of game and kids are going to see more and more of them in the future. Games are being used to teach reading and times tables and even science.

One of the first educational games I liked when I was little was called Lemonade, which is on the Elementary My Dear Apple disk. It shows you how to run a business by letting you set up and run your own lemonade stand. This was the best kind of educational game. You had fun playing and didn't even know you were learning at the same time.

Recently my brothers and I got a game that is a lot of fun. Much to our surprise, it is really educational, too, but we don't hold that against it. The game is called Microbe (by Synergistic Software).

This game was written by a programmer and a medical doctor, and is supposed to be good for even doctors to learn with. You are the commander of a submarine which has been miniaturized and injected into the bloodstream. You must travel to the brain and save the patient. Along the way you run into danger and medical emergencies that you must conquer. After you have played for a while, and gotten pretty good at navigating through the bloodstream and into the various organs, it suddenly occurs to you that you are also learning anatomy, health, medical terms and therapies.

If more educational games were like this, more kids would go out and buy them.

—Jared

string A series of characters making up a word or a sentence. Sooner or later, computers handle all information as numbers, but there has to be a way to tell the difference between numbers that mean letters of the alphabet and that have to be manipulated by one set of rules, and numbers that are just numbers and can be added, subtracted, multiplied and divided according to the familiar rules of arithmetic. Names, places, and things are all string variables in programs, and they are usually designated by a dollar sign. N$ is a string variable name, and so are P$ and T$. The computer would treat "N," "P," and "T" as numbers, however. If you enter a name when the program is expecting a number, the program will balk. If you do the opposite—enter a number when the program wants a string—it might accept the number but treat it like a string.

structured programming An approach to programming that involves extensive use of **subroutines**, and in general, writing the program so that it can be tested and **debugged** in pieces.

subroutine Segments of **programs** that are used more than once. Rather than keep writing the same code over and over again in order to, for example, calculate the balance in a checkbook program, the program can jump to the subroutine with a **GOSUB** statement, execute the instructions in the subroutine, and then jump back to the very next statement in the program after the GOSUB. The jump can be made from anywhere in the program, and the action will always return to the next instruction after that particular GOSUB. With **compiled** languages like **FORTRAN**, it is possible to have a whole library of separately compiled subroutines, which can be used by several different programs. Extensive use of subroutines is a feature of **structured programming**.

syntax In grammar, syntax is the set of formal rules governing the ways words are put together to make phrases and sentences, and the use of punctuation. The rules of syntax are very rigid in computer languages, and probably the most often seen phrase in all computing is "SYNTAX ERROR," meaning that you have done something like using a colon instead of a semicolon, or entering a letter when the computer was expecting a number.

systems analysis The planning and analysis that takes place, or should take place, before programming begins. The systems analyst figures out whether a particular situation will be improved by the use of computers, and by how much, and makes recommendations about the type of equipment and software that will be needed.

tape Magnetic tape for computer use is much like the ordinary audio tape for recording music. In fact, cassette players using common cassettes provide program and data storage for many low-cost computer systems; and if you play a computer cassette as if it were music, you will hear what sounds like regular bursts of static. Big computer systems use reels of inch-wide tape mounted on "tape drives." Movies that feature computers in some way usually show a room full of tape drives with their reels turning this way and that. The movement suggests action, and so we tend to think that the tape drives are the computers. Actually, computers themselves show about as much apparent activity as a rock. The whirling tape drives are selecting and retrieving data. Information is strung out along the length of the tape, so that to find any particular item on the tape, you have to **read** everything until you come to what you want. In terms of the time it takes to retrieve data from storage, even big tape drives are inefficient compared to **disk drives**, which can use **random access** to go directly to the needed data. Disks are generally used for storage of data that is needed frequently; and tape is used for less often needed data and for **backup** purposes, because it is economical for mass storage.

---

telecommunications Sending messages—usually between computers—over lines originally intended for telephone communications. There are many, many ways to do this, ranging in speed from the traditional, slow and fairly clumsy communications via teletype, at around ten characters per second, to the firehose rates possible with sophisticated equipment. Equipment ranges from the same telephone wires used by your mother to chat with her favorite sister, to giant dishes aimed at a satellite in orbit 26,000 miles above the earth. A whole branch of science devoted to this topic.

Telenet One of the commercial **packet switching** networks that enable the user of a computer on one side of the country to exchange information with or tap into a **database** on the other. By way of one of these services, a user can make a local phone call to the network, and be put in touch with a distant computer at very low cost in comparison with long distance rates. Telenet provides communications services to computers in the same way the long distance telephone companies provide voice service.

teletex A term that describes the use of **word processors** in combination with communications equipment. Messages can be efficiently prepared and edited on the word processor and then transmitted at relatively high speed by **MODEM** to another word processor or to a computer for storage and later retrieval by the addressee. Teletex is much faster and more flexible than traditional **Telex**. Sometimes this word is confused with **teletext**. (See also **electronic mail**.)

teletext Television pictures are broadcast one line at a time, with several hundred lines making up a picture, all in a fraction of a second. Teletext is a method of transmitting additional information in between the other lines, to be decoded at the receiver. The captions that appear on sets used by deaf people are transmitted this way, and those sets have special decoding equipment. Teletext transmissions are always in either text or cartoon form rather than camera images, and a number of information services, such as news, weather and classified advertising, are becoming available by this method.

Teletype Trademark of the Teletype Corporation, but generally used to describe any low-speed **terminal** whose main function is to send messages to similar terminals at around ten characters per second, usually with only upper-case letters available. Teletypewriters for sending cables and telegrams have been around a lot longer than computers, and were adapted to handle communications with computers when **interactive** programs were first being developed. Ten characters per second would be very fast for a person using a typewriter, but when the computer is capable of sending messages at hundreds of characters per second, a Teletype is a tortoise of a terminal.

Telex An Acronym for TELetypewriter EXchange Service of Western Union Corporation, Telex has come to mean the type of communications network used by slow-speed teletypewriters, and also the messages that are sent on them. International Telexes are often called "cablegrams," or just "cables."

terminal A railroad or bus terminal is at a point on a railroad or bus line where trips begin and end. A computer terminal is at the end of a cable or telephone line attached to a computer. It originates messages (usually by means of a keyboard like a typewriter's) and receives them (with a printer or video screen like a TV's). There are many kinds, including little ones the size of a calculator, and big department store cash registers that not only make change, but send all of the information about your purchases to a computer.

terminal software A program or programs that will make your personal computer behave like a **terminal** for purposes of talking to other computers.

Communication is one of the most complex aspects of computing, partly because there are so many different standards for things like **baud** rate, **half-** or **full-duplex**, **parity**, **stop bits**. A terminal program will help you set all of those elements to match the computer you wish to **access**, and it may also be able to remember and dial the right telephone numbers for you. (See also **smart terminal** and **dumb terminal**.)

text file A file used primarily for storing text or other sequential data, and sometimes called a **sequential file.** In it, the data is stored in no particular order, except for the order in which it is entered. It's like a blank piece of paper on which you write starting at the top and using every line, and for this reason it is a common form for word processing files. (See also **random binary file**.)

timesharing The simultaneous, **interactive** use of a computer by more than one person, and sometimes as many as several hundred. A computer is very fast. Communications speeds are quite slow, and people are even slower. This means that a computer will be idle a lot of the time while waiting for its last message to be transmitted to the user, and waiting for the user to decide what to do next, and waiting for the new instructions to be transmitted back to it.

Transmission speeds between the parts of a personal computer are pretty fast, but using a big computer through telephone lines can be awfully slow from the computer's point of view. Time-sharing allows the computer to be working for someone else with its **CPU**, while the fairly dull work of sending messages back and forth is handled by a small program. (See also **timeslice**, below.)

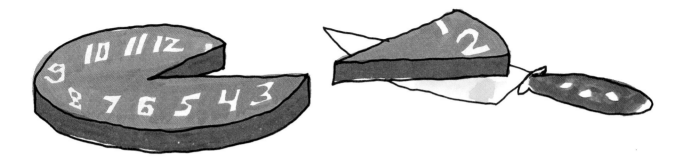

timeslice   The amount of the computer's time allocated in rotation to each user in a **timesharing** system. Imagine a teacher in a classroom full of children working on their different projects. The teacher might move from one to the next, spending a little time with each student while the others work on. The teacher would frequently check each child's progress, but as the number in the classroom increases, the time between any given student's checks goes up, too. Similarly, the computer's attention rotates among its several users, in strict order, spending a fraction of a second with each, but as the number of users goes up, **response time** goes up, too.

TOF   Stands for Top Of Form. When you start writing on a page, you automatically know where the top of the page is, and you allow margins at its top and bottom according to the kind of writing you are doing. A computer printer is usually dealing with continuous paper or with forms that are printed on only in certain spaces. It can't tell where one page ends and the next begins unless you tell it. TOF is often a button or switch on a printer that, when pressed, tells it that wherever it is typing now is the top of the page, or form. In any case, a printer normally assumes that TOF is whatever line the print head was on when it was turned on. Once the printer knows where TOF is, and how many lines of print are in the form, the computer can make the printer print anywhere on the page with great accuracy, over and over again, as long as the paper continues to feed in evenly. (See also **tractor**.)

toggle   A type of switch that has two positions, like the one that turns the lights on and off in your bedroom. You can "toggle" back and forth between light and dark. A toggle switch can also be used to switch between two different states, such as the fast and slow speeds on an electric mixer. In computer terminology, toggle can refer either to a familiar type of **hardware** switch, or to a **software** switch, such as between upper and lower case in a word processor.

trace A programming aid. A trace records the line numbers of a program in the order in which they are **executed**. This routine makes it possible to see if the steps the program is actually taking are the same ones that you expected, and whether they are being taken in the right order.

track The surfaces of **disks**, both hard and floppy, are divided into many concentric circles, called tracks; they are like the rings on a target, except that they are much closer together. A standard 5¼ inch floppy for a home or personal computer will have 35 or 40 tracks, and might have many more. The tracks are divided into **sectors**, and data is recorded sector by sector around the tracks. Each type of computer has a different standard for the number of tracks and sectors on a side and for how the data is actually to be recorded and then found again. The disks themselves might be transferable from one system to another of a different type, but whatever was on them would be unreadable. You might as well try to drive in Houston, using a map of Boston.

tractor A farm tractor hauls heavy wagons. A computer tractor is actually an attachment to the printer that hauls the paper through at a very precise rate. It has sprockets with little teeth that fit into the holes in the edges of the paper. A tractor feed is very useful if you expect to be printing out long reports or many copies, or at high rates of speed. The alternative is to feed the paper through rollers (platens) as on an ordinary typewriter: a process which is called "friction feed."

transient Something that happens for a while and then goes away. A transient **glitch** is a problem with either the computer or a program that does not  last long enough for you to find it and fix it, like the pain that goes away as soon as the doctor enters the room.

transistor A contraction of "transfer and resistor," actually the transfer of electricity across a resistor. Transistors are made out of specially treated silicon or germanium, and have the amazing property of being able to switch from conducting an electric current to resisting it in a fraction of a second, depending on the nature of the current. Transistors can also act as amplifiers of electrical signals, and that is how they are used in radios. In computers, transistors make up the arrays of **binary** switches that are the banks and circuits of memory and logic.

translator A program that translates from one natural (human) language to another, or from one high-level language (computer) to another. It is sometimes used to mean **compiler**, which is a program that translates from the **source code** of a computer language, such as FORTRAN, to its **object code**, the form in which the computer can really use it. (See also **interpreter**.)

tuple The usual way to describe an **array** or a table of data is by column and row, and the generally understood meanings of those terms are that the columns go up and down, and the rows are read across. Those terms can lead to confusion because in data processing, the contents of columns and rows may be switched about. To replace column and row, the terms "tuple" and "**vector**" have been adopted by some programmers because either can be assigned to a series of numbers without implying any particular direction on the page.

twisted pair A pair of wires that have been manufactured so that they twist around each other (in a long, double spiral, not tightly coiled). They are generally used for communications over fairly long distances, and the twisting helps to reduce the possibility of interference or **crosstalk** between one pair and others that might be nearby. (See also **coaxial cable** and **ribbon cable**.

Tymnet One of the major **networks** that enable users of computers and **databases** to communicate with each other across the country and internationally. The network belongs to Tymshare, Inc. Using Tymnet, like **Telenet**, involves making a local phone call to the network, and paying a quite low fee for use of it to access a remote computer. The networks generally do not offer computing services themselves, but instead act as data carriers for anyone wishing to arrange computer-to-computer communications.

UNIVAC An acronym for UNIVersal Automatic Computer. Introduced in 1954 by the General Electric Company, UNIVAC became famous as the first computer to be used in commercial data processing, although an earlier model had been being used by the Census Bureau since 1951. UNIVAC was designed by computer pioneers John W. Mauchly and J. Presper Eckert, Jr., whose company had been bought by Remington Rand Company in 1949. It was retired to the Smithsonian Institution after only 12 years of service, which gives you an idea of how rapid computer evolution was, even in the early years.

Unix An advanced, multi-user **operating system** developed at Bell Laboratories and now becoming available for some of the more powerful microcomputers, where it is known as **Xenix**. Operating systems manage storage on the disks and generally make sure that things happen in the right order among the various parts of the computer. Some of the other well-known operating systems for micros are **CP/M**, MS-DOS and DOS 3.3.

---

update To bring up to date; to add the latest information; to correct existing information or data with the latest available. Update is a word that comes out of the telegraph tradition of compressing several words into one. (See also **input**.)

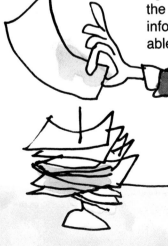

uptime Once you have come to rely on a computer to store data and do a lot of jobs that you used to do by hand but have now forgotten how to do by hand, the amount of time that the computer is available to you gets to be very important. Uptime is the number or percentage of hours per day that the computer is available and in working order. Major **timesharing** services maintain duplicate systems that can be switched in seconds to make sure that uptime is all of the time. (See also **downtime**.)

upward compatible One of the problems that computer users have is that whatever machine they have now, they will eventually outgrow, or they will want to add features to it that were not available when they first bought it. The worst part of the problem is that the programs that they have invested in and have gotten used to might not work on the new machines. A new machine with "upward compatibility" is one that can run programs originally designed for earlier machines of the same series—with little or no revision.

user, user-friendly The user is the person sitting at the **terminal** who is actually instructing or interacting with the computer; "user-friendly" describes programs that have been designed for use by people with little computer experience. They have plenty of instruction built into them. They have clear **error** messages and good **error recovery**, and the **documentation** that comes with them is accurate, clearly written and thoroughly indexed.

user group A group of people who all use the same kind of computer or computer program, and have organized to share information about how to use it better. Some groups are very formal, with meetings and publications; others are just informal networks of people who exchange information or back each other up in case of equipment failure. Computer users are often extremely generous with their special knowledge of the way things work, and it is an excellent idea to belong to a group that will let you share in that knowledge. Dealers usually know about local user groups that have organized around the products that they sell. Some user groups can be joined or consulted by logging onto **The Source** or **CompuServe** or one of the many **bulletin boards**.

utility A program or group of programs for performing housekeeping chores such as deleting, renaming or copying files or disks, or recovering damaged or mistakenly deleted files. Utilities are often part of the **operating system**, but there are many additional special utility programs available for almost every kind of computer.

validation Making sure that information is correct by testing it. **Passwords** are checked by comparing them to a list of users and determining that the password given is valid for the **files** of information that have been requested. Data can be validated by comparing it to a range of expected values and rejecting it if it falls outside that range. For example, date information can be validated by making sure that the month number is no greater than 12 and the day value is no greater than 31; or if the weight given for a six-year-old child is greater than, say, 100 pounds, the data ought to be checked again before being entered.

variable A name or a symbol that can have more than one value. In a simple equation such as $3X = Y$, both X and Y are variables. Any amount can be assigned to X, and that will result in a value for Y. Likewise, any amount can be assigned to Y, and that will yield a result for X. In programming, there are two basic kinds of variables—one for numbers, like X and Y in the example above; and the other for names and other alphabetical data. These are called **string** variables, or just "strings." If a program asks you for your name, it will store the answer as a string variable called something like "N$." (The dollar sign is used to identify a string variable.) When it asks you how old you are, it will store that answer as a numeric variable, like "A." The next person who uses that program will enter a different name and a different age, but the program will still use "N$" and "A" as its labels for the answers.

VDU Stands for Video Display Unit. VDU is a general term that can be applied to any display on a screen, whether it is a TV set or a **monitor**. This term is used mostly in England; in the United States, we generally refer to a CRT, or **Cathode Ray Tube**.

vector A term in mathematics used to describe a series of related numbers, such as the temperature of a certain room taken each hour of the day; or the scores of a whole class of children on a particular test; or the test scores of a single student over a whole year. A vector can be written as an **array**, in the form of either a column of figures or a row, whichever is most convenient. (See also **tuple**.)

videodisc A way of permanently storing information in **digital** form. Videodiscs are about the same size as phonograph records, but the data on them is recorded in concentric rings, like data on a computer's **hard disk** or **floppy**. Information can be stored on them and retrieved with **random access** techniques, in the form of either pictures or **binary code**. There are a few videodisc applications for microcomputers now, but the discs have such tremendous storage capacity that soon we may see applications such as an encyclopedia on a single disc.

videotex The internationally accepted term for **teletext**, in which textual information can be broadcast along with video images or on a separate channel, and then decoded by a special attachment to the television set.

Viewdata An information system developed by the British Post Office, now called "Prestel." It uses a combination of a telephone and a TV set to **access** a database of public information, from train schedules to movie and restaurant reviews, and from sports scores to election results.

virtual memory Many computer applications are limited by the amount of memory that is available inside the computer at any one time, such as 48K or 64K bytes. Virtual memory, or virtual storage, is a technique that enables a computer to treat its disk storage space as if it were an extension of its **internal memory**, by swapping sections of the program or files back and forth between the disks and internal memory as they are needed. It is a technique that is used on large **mainframe** computers as well as by some programs for micros.

VisiCalc Trademark of VisiCorp, for the most important program ever developed for a microcomputer. VisiCalc now has many imitators, but in 1978, it was the first "electronic spreadsheet" program. An electronic spreadsheet lets the user enter data in a **matrix** of columns and rows and then add, subtract, multiply and divide it in a way that makes it very easy to see what would happen to the whole calculation if any one number were to be changed. Businesses do a lot of this sort of thing in the process of budgeting and planning, and anyone who has had to do it by hand can understand the value of an electronic spreadsheet in about three minutes. VisiCalc, and the programs that imitated it, were responsible for the sales of lots and lots of microcomputers in business, which helped the whole market grow much faster than it might otherwise have.

VLSI Stands for Very Large Scale Integration. Integration is the process of manufacturing combinations of electronic parts all at once, on a single chip of silicon. VLSI refers to a scale of integration that puts as many as 10,000 transistors, or more, on a single tiny chip.

voice grade   Describes a telephone line that is adequate for transmitting telephone conversations, but which might be subject to various kinds of noise or **static**. We can tolerate some static while speaking, but it might interfere with high-speed data transmission.

Von Neumann machine   A kind of computer design that calls for all mathematical operations to be performed one step at a time, regardless of the nature of the problem or the data being worked with. This structure is based on the work of John Von Neumann, done at Princeton in the 1940s, and it is the way almost all computers work today. Other methods still in the laboratory involve breaking the problem into several pieces and working on them all simultaneously. (See also **parallel** processing.)

How to Program Inches into Bananas

My brother Colin and I teach an afterschool class in computer programming for kids. He is in high school now, and I am in the eighth grade. His first major programming project a few years ago was to teach me arithmetic and help me with my spelling. I still don't spell very well, but I go to computer camp and know some programming stuff he never heard of. Here is a little program that we worked out to start the kids out with. It is very simple, but shows a lot of important rules about programming in BASIC. Most of our students are in the third and fourth grades, and we teach the course at my school, The Village Community School, in New York City.

```
10 PRINT "WHAT IS YOUR NAME";
20 INPUT N$
30 PRINT
40 PRINT "HOW TALL ARE YOU IN INCHES, " N$;
50 INPUT X
60 PRINT
65 IF X < 30 OR X > 70 THEN 30
70 X = X * 2.54
80 PRINT
90 PRINT "YOU ARE ";X;" CENTIMETERS TALL."
```

First, program lines have to be numbered, usually in 10s, so that you can stick in things that you forgot about the first time through. The computer always executes the instructions in numerical order. Line 10 is called a print statement. If you want something to print out, you have to enclose it in quotes. It is followed by a semicolon, which makes the cursor pause on the same line to wait for the answer.

Line 20 makes a question mark appear after the word "NAME" and also stores the answer as N$. "N$" is what we decided to call the name. Since names are alphabetical, that input is called a string. Strings always have a dollar sign at the end. We can call this one "N-string" or "N-dollar."

Line 30 just makes the cursor skip a line so the output will be easier to read. Line 40 is another print statement, followed by a semicolon, followed by N$ and *another semicolon. Remember, the semicolons keep the cursor on the same line. N\$ stands for the name that was typed in, so at this point the computer makes that name print back.*

Line 50 is another input statement, only this time we are expecting a number for height in inches, and that gets stored in a variable name without the "\$," that is, one that can hold a number. The string N\$ and the number X are both variable names.

Line 60 just makes another blank line. Line 65 is called an IF statement. It is not really necessary in this program, and we usually leave it out until the kids have gotten the rest of the program working. What it does is check X to see if the number given is realistic for height. If X is not more than 30 inches or less than 70, the program goes back to line 30, skips a line, and asks the height question again. My brother and I don't want any students that are littler than 30 inches or taller than he is.

Line 70 does some work. It takes the value given for X and multiplies it by 2.54, the number of centimeters in an inch, and remembers the result as X, so the value for the X variable has changed within the program. This is a little confusing at first, but it happens all the time in programming. Line 80 is another blank line.

Line 90 prints the result. Notice how the semicolons and the quotes are arranged to make the result print out as a complete sentence, even though the variable X is in the middle of it.

When you run the program, it looks like this:

RUN
WHAT IS YOUR NAME? IAN

HOW TALL ARE YOU IN INCHES, IAN? 58

YOU ARE 147.32 CENTIMETERS TALL.

The kids have a lot of fun with this by putting in funny names and numbers for the variables and seeing what happens. One kid put in 7.5 instead of 2.54 on line 70, and then changed centimeters to bananas on line 90, so his program converted from inches to bananas! (At least it did after Colin reminded him to change the multiplication sign (*) to a "/" for division.) That's good, because it shows that the computer works only with the instructions and answers that are typed into it, and if a kid wants to call himself "Batman" or "Superwimp," or multiply when he means to divide, the computer doesn't know the difference, and doesn't care.

Then we tell them about line 65, which shows how some kinds of data can be checked to prevent mistakes, which is why we leave it out until the end. Without getting much more complicated than that kids can add a lot more questions and calculations to this program, about weight, distance, age, time and so on.

—*Ian*

WXYZ

Winchester drive   A **disk drive** that is small like a **floppy disk** drive, but fast and capable of holding large amounts of data like a **hard disk** drive. It is much less expensive than a regular hard disk drive, and can manage data in the **megabyte** range. Most individual users don't need that much storage space, but lots of businesses do. Small size and high reliability are accomplished by sealing up the disk part so that it can't be touched or damaged. This means that the disks can't be changed either, which also means that to make back-up copies of your data, you must have floppy disk drives or a **tape** drive, too. The Winchester Company does not make these drives. It makes guns, including a famous rifle called a 30-30. Instead the drive was developed at the **IBM** Corporation, and IBM used Winchester as a code name during the testing period. They did not want to use a more-descriptive name because it might give away the idea before they were ready to start selling the drives. One story is that the early versions were going to hold 30 megabytes of data on each side, so they were called 30-30s, after the rifle. Several companies now make this kind of drive, and they are all referred to as Winchesters or Winchester-types. Capacities range from about five megabytes to about 70, but the upper limit is constantly increasing, whereas their cost is steadily declining.

word   A logical unit of information, often equivalent to the ''byte size'' of the machine being used. For most home and personal microprocessors, a word equals a **byte** of eight bits, which is a confusing term because we also know that one byte is needed to encode one letter of the alphabet. Fortunately, ''word'' is not used very much in relation to the smaller computers that most of us start out on. It is more common with the larger ones, starting with the

IBM-PC, which has a 16-bit "microprocessor" and can work with a "word" of two bytes. **Mainframe** computers might use words of as many as eight bytes. Larger words generally mean faster processing.

word processing Probably the best reason for having a personal computer. Using a word processing program involves typing at a keyboard just as on a typewriter; but instead of the typed letters' appearing immediately on paper, they appear on the screen, where you have complete freedom to change them. You can easily insert new words, or sentences, or paragraphs in the middle of what you have already written, or you can delete material that you don't like. You don't have to read your own crabby handwriting, and you are free to try different ways of expressing an idea without ever having to erase anything or scratch it out, or copy over the parts that you are already satisfied with. When you have finished writing, you print out the results, and the computer keeps track of line length, paragraphing, pagination, centering titles, and all of the other elements of an elegant presentation of your work—even spelling. Word processing lets you concentrate on what you have to say; the computer takes care of how it looks.

word wrap When you come near the end of a line when using a typewriter, a bell or buzzer sounds; you can type a few more letters to finish a word, and then you use a carriage return lever or key to begin a new line. In most **word processing** programs, the carriage return action happens automatically. If you are in the middle of a word at that point, word wrap means that it also pulls that whole word down to the beginning of the new line. The only time you have to issue a return command is at the end of a paragraph.

write, write to The opposite of **read**, to send data from the computer to some form of storage, usually **disk** or **tape**, or to copy data from one storage device to another. Sending data to the printer is called "printing"; but sending it to the **monitor**, or screen, is also called printing. In computer terminology, you write data to the file or disk, and print to the screen or printer.

write protect Any of several methods for preventing the alteration of a computer **file** or **program** in storage. Music cassettes have little tabs that can be removed to prevent accidental re-recording. Diskettes in the 5¼ inch size have a little notch in their sides. Covering it with a bit of tape will prevent anything from being written to the diskette, while still permitting what's there to be **read**. The 8-inch floppies work in exactly the opposite way—covering the notch permits writing. It is also possible to protect the contents of individual files on a disk with a command to the **operating system** to lock a filename.

x-axis The horizontal axis on a graph. Think of a computer's screen or **monitor** as a piece of graph paper, with lots of lines from top to bottom and from side to side, or think of a wire screen for keeping mosquitos out of your bedroom. Picture each of the hundreds of squares formed by the wires crossing as a tiny light. Now think of being able to make patterns by turning on groups of those lights. That is how the computer makes patterns on the monitor or TV screen. The little "lights" are called **pixels**. Everything that happens on the screen is controlled by counting pixels from left to right and from bottom to top. The x-axis is the one you count from left to right, and the **y-axis** is from bottom to top. If the screen were 100 pixels wide and 100 high, the light at X50,Y50 would be in the middle; X5,Y5 would be in the lower left corner of the screen; and X95,Y5 would be at the lower right corner. Those references are called "coordinates," and all common graphs, whether on paper or on a screen, are drawn by finding coordinates along the x- and y-axes. Finding locations on a map is done the same way.

Xenix The microcomputer version of **Unix**, an **operating system** developed at Bell Laboratories for minicomputers—much larger than micros, but smaller than **mainframes**.

y-axis The vertical axis on a graph. (See also **x-axis**.) Everything that appears graphically on the screen of your computer is controlled by reference to imaginary up-and-down columns and side-to-side rows in the screen, just as if the screen were a map. The columns divide the x-axis, and the rows divide the y-axis.

Z-80 One of the most popular 8-bit microprocessor chips. It was developed by the **Zilog** Corporation in 1976, and it is still found in many different kinds of microcomputers, games (Pac-Man), and other "smart" electronic equipment. The popular **CP/M** operating system was developed for computers using the Z-80 and related chips as their microprocessors.

zap To destroy or delete something from memory. You can zap a file, or zap a program, or even zap a program or data out of **ROM**, something that is not normally done. "Zap" has the meaning of destroy rather than adjust or revise.

Zilog The company that introduced the very widely used **Z-80** microprocessor chip. It takes its name from "Z" for the last word, "i" for integrated, and "log" for logic — which translates to "the last word in integrated logic."

Zork Popular game of "adventure, danger, and low cunning," in the tradition of "Dungeons and Dragons." It features pure text—no arcade graphics. A description of the scene appears on the screen; and the player can react to it in various ways, scoring points for things found along the way, for successful encounters with various denizens, and for imagination and longevity.

Confessions of an Addict

Sitting alone in front of my computer, bathed in the monitor's green glow, I awoke to an unpleasant reality. I don't know when or how but somewhere along the line I had become a computer junkie. The symptoms had manifested over a period of months. Gradually and insidiously they had worked their way into my daily life and now I knew I would never be the same.

Oh, it began innocently enough, all right—a computer for my birthday, some educational software, a space war game. Maybe if I had stopped there it would have been okay, but that was just it, I couldn't stop! First came the games, the adventure games, the maze games, the shoot 'em up and knock 'em down games. I would buy almost anything with a fuzzy alien on the package. That, tragically, was only the beginning.

From software to hardware was no great jump in my condition. I started with another disk drive and then a printer. By counting pennies and counting days till Christmas I was also able to get joysticks and a color monitor. Each spare moment was spent in front of the computer. The desk on which it sat was usually littered with disks and Pepsi cans and the remains of long-forgotten meals. I did not consider dinner to be essential and would often skip it in favor of saving the galaxy with my joystick. Quite often I fell asleep at the computer when my eyes could no longer focus and my atrophied muscles wouldn't carry me to the bed. I would wake in the morning with the imprint of the keyboard on my cheek. I realized I was a bit obsessed but I felt I could quit if I wanted to. Maybe I could have if it hadn't been for that next fateful purchase, the MODEM.

I found myself no longer limited to whatever software I could collect; I could now tie in to other computers and computer junkies. The phone bills skyrocketed as I spent longer and longer talking to fellow enthusiasts and downloading programs. I developed friendships with people I had never seen by leaving messages on Bulletin Board Services while neglecting my non-computer friends.

Yes, I was a computer junkie and there was nowhere I could turn. No computers anonymous and no computer counselors. I was alone in the green glow of my monitor . . . a monarch with a whole new world at my fingertips.

—Colin